TEACH YOURSELF BOOKS

HOUSE REPAIRS

D0609881

A house must be kept in good repair if it is not to deteriorate
with age and depreciate in value. But calling in professional
labour to carry out the necessary maintenance and repair
work is an expensive business. There are many jobs that the
householder can do for himself, and this book shows him how
to tackle them. Clear instructions and diagrams are given
on repairing roofs, exterior walls, windows and doors, dealing
with damp, replastering and decorating interior walls, main-
taining floors and ceilings, and on a variety of other jobs
that arise in and around the house over the years. It deliberately avoids major constructional work, which is still best
left to the professional man.

TEACH YOURSELF BOOKS

HOUSE REPAIRS

Tony Wilkins

Editor, Do It Yourself Magazine

ST. PAUL'S HOUSE   WARWICK LANE   LONDON EC4P 4AH

First printed 1970
Second impression 1973

ISBN 0 340 05624 X

Printed and bound in Great Britain
for The English Universities Press Ltd by
Hazell Watson and Viney Ltd, Aylesbury, Bucks

Contents

1 Introduction

The greatest financial outlay the average family makes in a lifetime is that which involves the purchase of a home. This usually means the repayment of thousands of pounds spread over 25 years or more—during which time the property can become a valuable asset or a liability, depending upon the family living in it.

Like all material possessions, a house deteriorates with age if left alone. Rain, frost, pollution in the air and high winds all combine to spoil decorations and attack the actual fabric of the house. And the longer the period of neglect, the greater will be the expense of putting things right.

If kept in first class condition, time has already proved that a house is a big financial asset. Improvements and extensions are investments where much of the outlay will be recouped in the higher value of the house.

The greatest single factor when it comes to getting maintenance and repair work done to your home is the cost of professional labour. Couple this with the problem of finding professionals who take a pride in their work and pinning them down to a time, and the average man realises that it may be well worthwhile trying the work himself—even if it does take twice as long.

If you are thinking along these lines, this book is designed to help you tackle many of the jobs likely to be encountered in the average home over the years. It deliberately avoids the major constructional jobs still best left to the professional man. And it doesn't offer you an applied course in building. You can find such information in other books in this series.

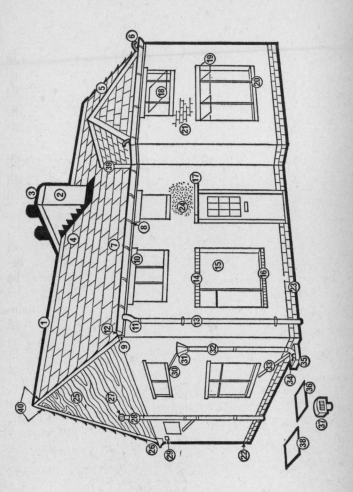

1. Ridge tiles
2. Chimney
3. Flaunching
4. Stepped flashing
5. Hip
6. Hip iron
7. Eaves gutter
8. Gutter bracket
9. Fascia
10. Concrete lintel
11. Swan neck
12. Stop end
13. Down pipe
14. Soldier arch
15. Picture window
16. Brick-on-edge sill
17. Canopy
18. Horizontal pivot sash
19. Top-hung casement
20. Tiled sill

21. Facing bricks
22. Damp proof course
23. Brick plinth
24. Pebble dash or rough cast
25. Waney edge boards
26. Finlock concrete gutter
27. Wire or plastic cage
28. Soil and vent pipe
29. Air brick
30. Bath waste pipe
31. Hopper head
32. Main waste pipe
33. Sink waste pipe
34. Down pipe shoe
35. Gully
36. Inspection chamber
37. Fresh air inlet
38. Interception chamber
39. Valley
40. Roof verges

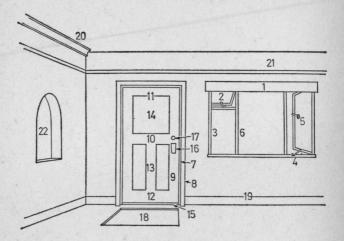

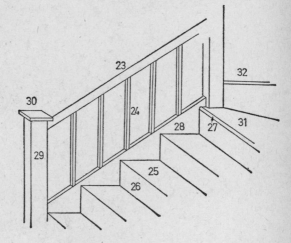

1. Pelmet
2. Opening light
3. Jamb
4. Casement stay
5. Cockspur
6. Mullion
7. Lining
8. Architrave
9. Stile
10. Middle rail
11. Top rail
12. Bottom rail
13. Muntin
14. Panel
15. Threshold
16. Finger plate
17. Door furniture
18. Mat well
19. Skirting
20. Coving or cornice
21. Picture rail
22. Wall niche
23. Hand rail
24. Baluster or banister
25. Tread
26. Riser
27. Nosing
28. String or stringer
29. Newel post
30. Newel cap
31. Winder
32. Half landing

The first essential, when you decide to be your own repair man, is to build up a kit of good quality tools. Of course there is a financial outlay, but good tools will more than last a lifetime, and you will probably save their cost over the first couple of years' work. You will find details of tools in chapter 13.

Today, in most areas, you don't need to spend good money on larger specialised tools which you may use only occasionally. There are hire companies whose sole job it is to supply well maintained tools and equipment to the handyman for a reasonable daily or weekly hire charge. In this way you can have the benefit of, say, a scaffold kit, steam wallpaper stripping machine or a floor sander for a reasonable outlay, knowing it will be back in the shop in a few days. If you can do your own collecting and returning, you will reduce the cost quite a bit.

And do make use of the mass of literature available to the do-it-yourself man today. Manufacturers spend a fortune on producing it, and usually it is yours for the asking. Similarly, there are many Associations willing to offer advice and information, just for the asking. You will find some of these listed at the end of chapter 13.

You may well find that in other literature and books you refer to, quite a number of semi-technical words are used for parts of your home. To help simplify matters, the illustrations introduce some of the terms used about a house exterior, and some of those found indoors. Even if you don't memorise them, then they can be referred to when required.

Before turning to actual maintenance work, there is a final consideration: safety. This will be stressed throughout the book, but it is worth repeating here.

Always use the correct tools for the job, and use them in the manner recommended by the maker. When working above the ground, use a safe method of reaching—whether merely a pair of steps to reach the top of a cupboard or a roof laddder to get to a chimney pot. If there is the slightest question of one person being unable to cope—such as when removing a heavy fire surround, or climbing steps on un-even ground, call in help. Don't lift things too heavy for you—even if the man who delivered them managed on his own. And don't take risks with electrical appliances, plugs or sockets.

Bearing safety in mind—have a go. Tens of thousands of people over recent years have found that the only thing which stopped them doing jobs about the home was lack of confidence in their own ability.

2 Roof Level

The fact that the roof is well out of normal reach does not mean it stays in sound condition. High winds, frost, heaped snow and ice and slight structural movement may well have attacked the fabric and dislodged mortar, flashings and roof coverings.

One method of superficially checking for damage is to stand across the road with a pair of binoculars. Examine the chimney pots; the mortar bed on which they stand; the state of the pointing; the flashing which bridges the gap between chimney stack and the roof. Look for displaced or cracked slates or tiles, and for sagging or otherwise damaged gutters.

This offers, of course, a very limited check, and it should not replace a regular check at roof level.

The first problem to overcome is safe access to the roof. To reach a gutter, you need an extension ladder which offers at least three rungs above gutter level so there is something to grip at the top. Make sure the ladder is angled correctly, and it must be anchored at the base to make sure it cannot slip. It is wise to anchor the top as well, for if the ladder is rested on modern plastic guttering, it tends to slide sideways very easily.

While the ladder gets you up to the roof, it does not present very comfortable working conditions, so if there are jobs to do involving quite a time, two ladders with a plank suspended between on decorators' cripples, or a handyman-type scaffold kit will prove invaluable. It is still wise to have a ladder to give access to a scaffold.

Alternatively, there is a simple scaffold kit which leans

against the wall, and across which can be rested scaffold
boards. These should always be the real thing, and not odd
pieces of wood found in the shed. Wherever possible, erect
a safety rail to hang on to—especially if you are not used
to heights.

If you need to get up to the chimney stack, borrow or
hire a proper roof ladder. This has wheels on one side so
you can manoeuvre it in place, and a large shaped frame on
the other side which, when the ladder is turned over, sits
neatly and securely over the ridge. If the bottom is then
lashed to the top of your ladder or scaffold, you will have
safe access to the stack.

Assuming you have to work on the roof, start right at the
top. Examine the pots for cracks. If a pot has to come
down, it must be roped and lowered. Don't trust yourself
carrying it down, because of the weight. Look also at the
mortar on which the pots stand, called the flaunching.
Loose material should be dug away with a trowel point, the
gap brushed out, then damped with water and new mortar
applied with a small trowel.

In most places you can buy dry mortar mix in paper
sacks ready for mixing with water. While this does work
out dearer for large jobs, it certainly saves buying more
than you need for smallish jobs. Don't mix more at a time
than you can use in about half an hour. And keep the mix
fairly dryish so it doesn't slop all over the place and mark
the brickwork.

Look at the pointing of the chimney stack, and rake out
all loose and crumbling mortar and re-point with a mortar
mix after damping all gaps. There is a good reason for damping, for the added moisture prevents water being drawn
from the new mortar mix, thus weakening it before it has
time to harden.

In some older properties you may find the chimney stack
in pretty poor shape—very often caused by corrosive
materials deposited on the flue lining. When damped by rain
or condensation, the chemicals attack the flue lining, and

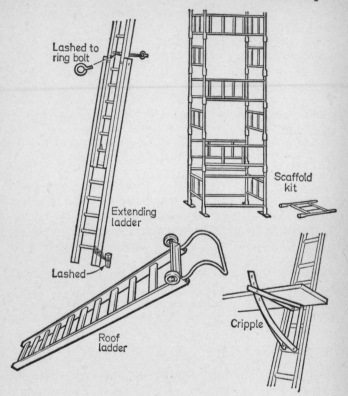

Lashed to ring bolt

Extending ladder

Lashed

Roof ladder

Scaffold kit

Cripple

eventually the mortar between the brickwork, often distorting the stack until it is dangerous. If you encounter this, call in professional help, for a very considerable weight of masonry is being dealt with. Should the stack topple, it could do a lot of damage on its way down! And, anyway, special chimney scaffolding is necessary for rebuilding.

Examine the flashing where chimney stack and roof join. You will see a material, usually lead, but in some modern cases fibre, which has been let into the pointing in sort of step-form. This sometimes pulls away, and if it has, the joints concerned should be raked out, the flashing pushed in and wedged with spare bits of scrap lead, then new mortar applied.

If rips or tears are encountered, a bitumen mastic is useful for repair work. This can be trowelled into small cracks, but if larger areas are involved, a piece of coarse sacking or scrim can be worked into the area by rubbing the mastic over it. The material affords a base and a key for the mastic, and when set, you can put on a further protective coat.

In really bad cases the flashing may have to be cut out and replaced. Instead of traditional lead, get some Nuralite flashing, which is far easier for the beginner to use. You can get instructions on its use with the product.

Now move down to the seeming acres of roof covering! In older properties, slates may have been used, and these are held in place on the tiling laths by nails. Rustless nails should be used, but in many cases they were not, and when nails rust through, the slates can slide away. It is not easy to re-nail, so if you do encounter a slipped slate, make up a simple clip from zinc or similar rustless metal. Slide and hook the slate in place.

If the house is fairly old, you may be able to see the slates from the loft, and this makes fixing much easier. If you encounter a cracked slate, the bitumen mastic already mentioned will effectively seal the gap. Where a temporary repair is necessary use a mastic glazing tape pressed in place. An epoxy resin type filler paste such as is used for car body repair work will also deal with cracks.

Where tiles are encountered, whether of clay or cement, you will find the method of securing is different. Nibs on the tile hook over the tiling laths, then every third or fourth course is usually nailed with rustless nails to prevent lifting. Where high winds are encountered, even more nailing is advisable.

It may be possible to replace a slipped tile by pushing it

back until the nibs re-locate with the correct lath. If it
won't hold in place, a small amount of mortar will do the
trick—or, if access from underneath is possible in the loft,
the tile may be held by a strip of glass fibre repair material.
In more modern properties, the roof will be what is called
'felted', which means that a heavy duty felt is laid between

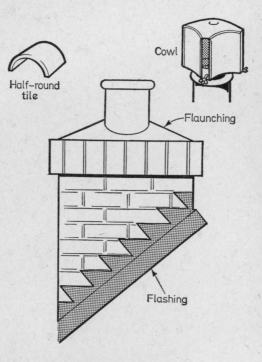

tiles and the rafters. If this is the case in your home, you
will not be able to get at the tiles from inside.

Also, in older properties, you may find that every gap
between tiles has been sealed with mortar—which inevit-
ably seems to disintegrate and drop out.

This is technically known as pargeting, and if it is damaged, there is nothing for it but to rake out all the damaged mortar and replace it with a new, fairly weak, mix, to which has been added a quantity of pva emulsion. This acts as an adhesive, and it will help to ensure the mortar does not drop out so easily next time. It must be borne in mind that this replacement will be a long and tedious job.

You may also encounter mosses and lichens growing on your tiles, in which case, buy a fungicide and treat the

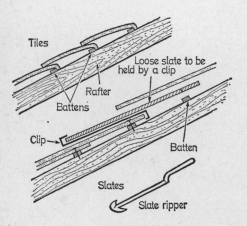

affected tiles to kill off any growth. A stiff brush used dry will remove the worst before the chemical is applied.

At gutter level, the first job is to clear out all rubbish—leaves, nests and moss—with a small trowel, then brush clean. You will then be able to spot any damage. In older properties, gutter brackets may have loosened under the weight of snow and ice. Tighten the screws, or if they won't tighten, use a larger screw—or fill the existing hole with a plastic wall plug and re-fix. While this is being done, it is a good idea to check the fall of the gutter towards the down pipe by pouring a can of water into the gutter at the point farthest from the down pipe. It should all flow away. If it gathers at any point, it may mean a bracket or two needs slight adjustment.

Look for areas of rust, and see if the gutter has rusted through. A vigorous sweep with a wire brush will soon show any damage, but be sure to protect your eyes from flying rust. You can buy protective glasses—or use motor cycle goggles. Repair holes with a resin paste filler; larger ones with a glass fibre repair material. Joints between sections can be sealed with a bitumen mastic material trowelled on and left to set.

Look for nests in the tops of down pipes and hook them out upwards—don't push them down. A nest swollen by damp can form a very effective blockage at a point difficult to reach. When the pipes are clear, fit wire or plastic

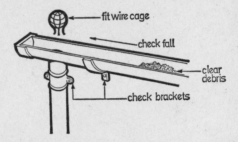

cages to the tops to prevent further trouble. Or fit strips of special plastic mesh over the guttering. These can be clipped in place. They will keep leaves and other debris out too—but having fitted cages, you must see that leaves don't so block the cages that water cannot get away.

Sometimes you will find gaps where one down pipe slots into the next. It is best not to seal these gaps, as they act as effective tell-tales should a blockage occur in a pipe. Water will come out of the joint immediately above the blockage. If the pipe has been sealed, water will have to overflow from the top, giving no indication where the trouble has occurred.

Before repainting gutters and down pipes, rub off all loose rust with wire brush and emery paper. Wipe clean then treat

the rusted area with a rust inhibitor to neutralise it. When
dry, re-paint. For the interior of the gutters, use up any left-
overs of good quality exterior paint, regardless of colour.
No one will see it but the birds! Often, a dullish brown or
black bituminous paint is used, in which case you will have
to use bituminous paint again, as it bleeds through normal
paint coatings applied over it.

It is a good idea to hold a piece of cardboard to the wall
when painting down pipes so you don't mark the brickwork.
And if you feel really energetic, apply a coat of paint to the
inside of each down pipe. Again, left-overs can be used, and
it can be applied—or spread—by tying a heavily weighted
piece of towelling to an old rope and lowering it into the
pipe. The towelling should be a fair fit in the pipe so that
when paint is poured on the towel it can be rubbed on to
the pipe surface. Don't lose the weight in the pipe!

Where previous paint is sound on gutters and pipes, all
you need do is rub over with a pumice or stripping block
damped in water to take down the gloss and afford a key
for the new paint. Wash over with clean water and allow to
dry. Where paint is flaking or blistering, it should be
stripped off, either by blowlamp or chemical stripper, down
to bare metal, then re-painted. You can read more about
painting in chapter 4.

Remember that bare metal will quickly rust again if
left unprotected, so don't strip off more paint than can be
replaced before the day's work is done. This probably
means you need a plan of campaign to split the work into
easily managed sections.

3 Exterior Walls

The outer walls of your house will be one of two types—solid or cavity. The solid wall is found in older properties going back before the 1930s, and, in fact, at one time all walls would naturally be solid, and perhaps of considerable thickness. The snag is that, given time, damp can strike through from the outside to the inside—especially if the mortar becomes porous with age. One big advantage of the solid wall is that it tends to be warmer in winter and cooler in summer—providing it is dry.

The more modern exterior wall consists of two complete walls separated by a gap or cavity. The two walls are in fact bonded together by means of wire or sheet metal wall ties, and these are designed so that water cannot pass from one leaf of the wall to the other. So, in theory, the cavity prevents the outer wall, perhaps soaked by rain, coming into contact with the inner wall, which therefore remains dry.

Where the system fails, it is usually the fault of careless building. Mortar droppings from bricklaying drop on to and bridge some of the wall ties, and in damp weather the mortar acts as a wick, passing moisture from one wall to the other, and appearing as damp patches indoors.

We still associate brick with house construction, and to a certain extent this is correct. Most older properties are of brick construction—apart from certain country districts where local stone has been put to good use. But today methods of construction are changing. It is still quite common to use an attractive brick for the outer leaf of a wall, but to build up the inner wall of lightweight blocks or a kind of hollow tile, both of which speed up construction consi-

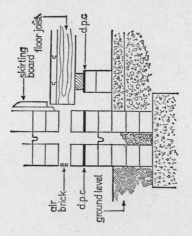

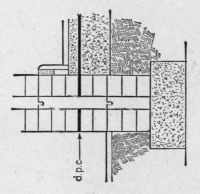

derably. You will soon discover any divergence from normal materials when you come to drill holes in the wall. With many lightweight blocks, you can in fact knock a nail in as you would into a piece of wood. But with the hollow blocks they are extremely hard to drill—then suddenly the masonry drill disappears into a cavity!

Or it may be that your home has two walls of lightweight blocks, with the outer clad with timber, tiles, wood shingles or plastic planking. It will be up to you to discover just what

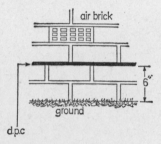

you have got so you can figure out how to deal with problems.

Assuming your walls are of brick or block—or both—remember that even good quality bricks are designed to be porous to a certain degree. Rain hitting the brickwork will be absorbed a little, then, when the rain has stopped, the moisture will dry out. This is quite normal, and in most cases this has no effect on the weatherproof nature of your home. But where bricks are old and porous, or where poor quality bricks have been used, the absorption may be too great, and damp may be carried through to the house interior.

Moving closer to the ground, you will find that in modern homes there is some form of horizontal barrier around the house in a continuous layer. This is called the damp proof course, and it is designed to prevent water in the ground rising freely up the walls. The d.p.c., as it is often called, consists of a layer of special bitumen felt, plastic slate or other impervious material bedded into a course of brickwork at least 6 inches above ground level. Thus damp is kept below all timberwork and decorations at all points.

Also at about d.p.c. level you will see in the average house airbricks spaced around the walls. These are put there to allow air to pass under a house, thus ventilating the space below a timber ground floor. It is essential that air is allowed to move freely, and on no account should the air bricks be covered up. Dry rot spores are always present in the air, and they only normally get a grip in dank, unventilated areas. They don't like fresh air on the move!

Of course, if your home has solid walls and solid floors, you probably won't find any air bricks, so the above precaution does not apply.

Wall Problems

If an exterior wall is too porous, heavy rain may, as has already been said, soak in too far and find a way to the inner wall. This may be caused by porous bricks, decaying pointing or both, so examine the offending wall some hours after rain. If it still looks soaking wet, the bricks may well be waterlogged. Examine the pointing and try digging at it with a tool such as a large nail bent to form a rough rake. Dig out all loose and crumbling material to a depth of $\frac{1}{2}$ inch to $\frac{3}{4}$ inch, then brush out with an old paint brush.

For re-pointing, you can buy a good pre-mixed mortar by the bag, which only needs water adding. When you mix it, keep the mortar on the dry side. A sloppy mix will run down the brickwork causing marks which are hard to remove. Before applying the mortar, damp the cavities with water applied by the old paint brush. This prevents the brickwork drawing moisture from the new mortar, thus weakening it.

Check how surrounding pointing is finished off. It may be flush, weathered or hollow. You can achieve the flush or weathered effect with a trowel and a little practice, but the

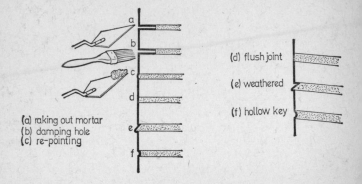

(a) raking out mortar
(b) damping hole
(c) re-pointing

(d) flush joint

(e) weathered

(f) hollow key

hollow is best done with a piece of metal rod pressed into the joint and drawn along.

Should you spill mortar on the brickwork, you can buy a concrete solvent at most large builders' merchants, and this can be used to remove the mortar without affecting the bricks. You can also use the liquid for cleaning tools and plant on which the concrete has set. Do read the instructions on the can very carefully, for the material is acid, though quite harmless if used correctly.

To correct the over-porous wall, coat it with one of the excellent water repellents now available. Some are silicone-based, some are not; but the effect is to seal off the wall surface yet still allow the bricks to 'breathe'. This means that any water vapour in the wall can escape, but rain cannot get in. Most repellents contain a special dye which enables you to see where you have been, but which, after a week or so, disappears, leaving a completely transparent film. Again, follow the instructions carefully, and don't skimp on solution if they tell you to flood the surface.

Try to keep repellents off paintwork, for even if they do no harm in themselves, they can produce splash marks on grubby paint which are hard to move.

Damp patches indoors at skirting level usually mean a

faulty damp proof course—or no d.p.c. at all! Putting in a
new strip one can be done by cutting out small sections of
a horizontal joint and inserting new sheeting, but this is not
the easiest of jobs and a special saw is needed. The simplest
amateur treatment is to use a special damp resisting liquid
which has the ability to soak into the wall up to a depth of
9 inches.

It rather resembles petrol in nature (and there the resem-
blance ends)—but it does soak very readily into brickwork,
and once in, no damp can pass it. An interior grade is produced too, and between the two, a very effective d.p.c. is produced.

If you prefer professional help, there are two or three
different treatments available, ranging from liquids fed into
prepared holes to what is called the Electro-Osmosis
system where the electrical potential of a damp wall is
short-circuited by means of special copper strips very effectively earthed.

While nothing is seen to happen, and nothing is connected to an actual electrical supply, it has been proved
that damp moves down and out in a most remarkable
fashion.

Yet another system works by means of small angled tubes
set in the wall, out of which moisture flows from a damp
wall. All the above are professionally applied, and your
local telephone books will indicate companies able to help.

Apart from structural faults, sheer carelessness may
cause trouble at d.p.c. level. Earth heaped above the d.p.c.
will allow moisture to by-pass it—so watch out for the level
of rockeries, heaps of sand or other building materials close
to house walls. The building of new paths may also cause
trouble if the path gets too close to the d.p.c. Rain bounc-
ing up will then splash above the d.p.c. where it cannot of
course soak down. The cure here is either to lower the level
of the path—which is usually a major operation—or to
build a skirting or plinth. This must be made of cement
containing a waterproofing agent, making the concrete

quite impervious to water. Such waterproofing agents are available in powder form from a builders' merchant, and they should be added to the dry mix prior to adding the mixing water. The skirting may then extend above d.p.c. level, preventing splashes getting at the wall.

Even the application of a water repellent or liquid d.p.c. will help if you don't fancy going to too much trouble.

Cracks in walls should be checked too. If yours is a newish house there may be settlement in the foundations in the first few years. However slight, this can cause stresses in brickwork, resulting in minor cracks at weak points such as between window openings and the ground. Usually all you need do is re-point, or add a little dry colour to the mortar to match the brickwork—and that's the end of it.

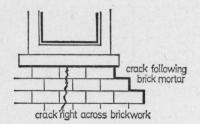

crack following
brick mortar

crack right across brickwork

But in just a few cases, where settlement is severe, or where ground has been undermined, cracking may continue. You can carry out a simple test by bridging cracks at a number of points with dabs of mortar or plaster. Check over the months, and these 'tell-tales' will indicate whether movement is continuing. If it is, you would be wise to con-sult your borough surveyor, through the local town hall, and ask his advice. Underpinning of foundations is not a job for the amateur.

If your home is built on clay, you may suffer from minor movement which does not rate as serious—but more as annoying. During summer months the clay dries and shrinks, then during the wetter months the clay expands and swells—possibly causing movement in the house built on it. In this case, cracks may open and shut according to the season—and this may be noticed indoors and out—and where one building adjoins another, such as lean-to garage and house.

Exterior walls can be finished in a number of ways, any of which may need attention at some time or other.

Decorative brick is pretty well self-cleaning. If it does look jaded, it can be improved by raking out pointing and repointing to give a fresh appearance. Bricks should be cleaned by stiff brush and clean water. Never add detergents or soap to the water, for this will leave streaky marks which cannot later be removed. If you have a spare brick of the same type as the wall, you can break the brick and use a piece to rub down the brickwork.

Some older properties have plain rendered walls, which can look very dull. Such walls can be treated with a good stone or cement paint. First wash down the walls with clean water, rake out all cracks and fill with mortar. When dry, apply the paint as directed with as wide a brush as you can get. The advantages of such paints are that they will fill any minor irregularities in the wall surface, and add an attractive texture to an otherwise bare area. Don't over-do the colour on large areas, for what looks good on a shade card can look hideous on a complete wall. Stick to naturals or white.

If the rendering is in good shape, there are other paints you could use. A whole range of reinforced paints are now available, with such materials as mica or nylon fibres added to a good quality plastic paint to add durability and be gap-filling. Exterior grade emulsion paint will also give long protection, but it may show up irregularities. Thinner paints can be applied by paint roller, and for exterior surfaces the wool pile type is best as it lasts well and gets into cracks and crevices.

Whichever paint you use, it pays to spread dust sheets or sacking over paths and flower beds, low roofs and porches.

Paint splashes, once dry, can ruin an otherwise attractive
job.

In many other cases, the exterior rendering has been em-
bellished before setting. Small stones or chips of rock may
have been thrown on to give a pebbledash or spar dash
effect. Or the top coat of rendering may have been flung on
from a special machine called a Tyrolean Projector. Most
of these finishes last well, and need very little cleaning. The
most you can do to freshen them is wash down with a garden hose. Rubbing or brushing may pull away the stones.

Some areas are exposed to the full force of winds and
rain, and these conditions plus, perhaps, a weak rendering,
result in large blisters which break, leaving bare patches in
the dash. It is not easy to repair these areas, and if the wall
is in pretty poor shape, it may be necessary for the whole
wall to be stripped and re-rendered. But if just small areas
are affected, cut away the damaged area with club hammer
and steel chisel.

As far as possible, collect up the stones which are cut
away, for it is very difficult to match well weathered ones.
You will find the wall has an under-coat of rendering, over
which is the coat which had the stones flung into it. If this
under-coat is sound, merely scratch across it with a trowel
to afford a key; damp it well down, and apply new rendering. This should consist of 1 cement, 1 sand, 1 lime mix, to
which has been added a quantity of pva emulsion. The latter adds an adhesive quality to the mix.

When ordering materials, tell your builders' merchant
what job you have on hand, and he will see that you get the
right kind of sand and lime.

The new rendering is applied by trowel and float to the
bare areas, bringing it flush with the surrounding rendering,
then the stones are loaded on a shovel and thrown smartly
on to the wet mix. Put sacking below the area to catch the
stones which don't stick, pick them up and fling them again
—and so on until the patch is covered. If you have to buy
new stones, be sure to take along a handful of old ones for

matching to avoid colour clashes. And before the stones are used, wash them to clean off dust. Keep them wet until you throw them on the wall.

If the wall is in a very exposed position, it may be as well to use a stronger rendering. Use a 1 cement, 3 sand mix, to which has been added some pva adhesive.

If the rendering is off down to bare brick, the same mix— with or without mortar according to conditions—should be used, for the undercoat as for the top coat.

If you wish to make plain rendering more attractive, the Tyrolean finish is well worth considering. The Tyrolean Projector, already referred to, can be hired from many hire shops for a reasonable fee, and the method of use is very quickly picked up.

Many modern homes have an area faced with timber— very often cedar—which can look most attractive. Unfortunately, untreated timber left to weather soon loses its lovely rich, warm colour, and it ends up an indifferent grey. To prevent this, the application of one of the cedar finishes is advisable, followed by a freshening coat every couple of years. Such finishes contain a pigment resembling cedar in colour, and this ensures the colour of the wood remains stable.

Very considerable development work is being done to produce really durable transparent finishes for exterior use. At the time of writing, the most hardwearing for external use is, in my opinion, good quality yacht varnish.

Cedar shingles can also be preserved in a similar manner, and regular treatment will ensure that they don't curl or split through drying out. Any misplaced ones should be re-fixed with rustless nails. If you can get them, use aluminium ones.

Where walls look really poor, you can re-face with vertical tiling, some of which is available in brick bond finish. Such a cladding can transform an old house, and greatly improve its weather resistant qualities.

4 Windows and Doors

Wherever there are openings in your house structure—such as at windows and doors, you will get attack by weather. And as with most maintenance work, it is wise to tackle damage as soon as you spot it, before the weather gets under protective layers. If there is no damage, a regular wash down of all painted surfaces will keep grime from ruining the paint surface. Pollution in the air can be very corrosive, especially in our larger towns.

Let's look at windows first.

Metal casement windows are common in many modern homes, and all good ones have been treated against corrosion before installation by galvanizing. In this case you should get little trouble even if paint is damaged. But in some older properties you may encounter metal windows that definitely are rusting through poor priming or lack of protection at factory stage.

Where you meet rusting, remove all surrounding paint with a scraper or, if necessary, with a chemical stripper. A blowlamp is effective, but unless you have some experience, be very careful, for you can easily crack the glass. It is essential to find the edges of any rusting, for if you miss a hidden area, it can continue to rust under any new coat you may apply.

Rub down the rust with wire brush and emery paper to remove all loose and flaking material, then treat the rusted area with a rust inhibitor, or with a cold galvanizing paint. When this has dried, you can apply metal primer to all other bare areas, then apply an undercoat. An undercoat is a full-bodied paint with obliterative powers, and it also provides a keyed surface for a finishing coat.

When the undercoat has dried, rub lightly with fine glass-paper, but go carefully or you will be back to bare metal. This rub is only to remove any specks of dirt or dust and level any streaks.

Finally apply two coats of gloss paint. This has less covering power than undercoat, but it has a much more durable surface. Never try to cover another colour with just top coat. It rarely will.

You can use one of the new one-coat paints in place of undercoat and top coat, and for this you don't brush out as for a normal paint—it is laid on rather thickly. You will find the paint is jelly by nature—known as thixotropic—and as you brush it out the paint thins, then it stiffens again. Even so, you may find the one-coat paint needs two coats to cover properly.

If your metal window frames are covered with sound paint and you merely wish to re-paint, don't strip it off. Merely wash down with a strongish solution of sugar soap or similar cleaner to remove all grease and grime, and to flat down the gloss slightly. Then repaint with gloss. If a new colour has been chosen, you will need undercoat to obliterate the old colour.

Of course there is a limit to the number of new coats that can be applied before the window starts to jam. If your windows are tight, you may have to strip off the paint coatings and start again.

Where rust has got a hold on metal frames, you may find the pressure exerted is enough to crack the glass in frames. Here, the glass will have to be removed, the rebates cleaned out and the rust rubbed off; the frame treated with rust inhibitor, then the glass replaced or renewed.

Where you find a frame is buckled and not seating properly, there is no simple solution. The faulty component really needs unbolting, the frame lifting out, the glass removing, the frame straightening—then the process reversed.

Sometimes metal windows are very hard to open and

close. First, try a little easing oil on joints. If this fails, loosen off the bolts holding the frame in place by just a fraction. You should find this does the trick. Or you may find the hinges are clogged with old paint. Apply paint stripper, strip off the paint, and re-coat, being careful to avoid clogging the hinge pins.

Timber Windows

You will meet two main types of wood window. The case-ment frame, which swings open on hinges, and the sash frame, which slides up and down. Most modern homes have casement, and very many of our older homes have sashes.

Ignoring the differences for a moment, if you examine paintwork and find it sound, to renew it all you need do is wash down with a sugar soap solution, remove the gloss with a pumice block dipped in water (sometimes called a stripping block) and wash down with clean water. The sur-face may then be top coated if you are working in the same colour, or undercoated if you are changing the colour.

Where you meet very slight damage, such as flaking areas over a limited area, strip off all loose material and rub down with glasspaper. Keep it fine or you will scratch surround-ing paint. If you are through to bare wood, apply fairly thin primer to the bare areas. Allow to dry then apply undercoat. When dry, give a very careful rub with fine glass-paper to remove any nibs. Finally, apply two coats of top coat, bringing the newly painted areas flush with the sur-rounding work. You can then re-coat all the paintwork as for normal repainting.

Where the paintwork is obviously in a bad way, it must be stripped off down to bare wood. The safest way for the amateur is by chemical stripper, but a blowlamp or blow-torch is effective in careful hands—and it is far cheaper providing you don't crack the glass! It is unwise to use a blowlamp in very cold weather where the glass temperature will be very low, thus giving a high temperature contrast.

When paint is softened, a scraper can be used for broad

areas, and a tool called a shave hook for angles and moulding. Wire wool is useful for dealing with difficult shapes.

With the paint off, read on the stripper bottle or can how
to neutralise the chemical and do this job carefully or you
may affect any new coating. Allow the wood to dry, then
rub down with fine glasspaper, being sure to work with the
wood grain. Dust off, then, if you can get one, use what is
called a tacky cloth to pick up all remaining dust. This is
a resin-impregnated cloth which is just sticky enough to
hold dirt but not sticky enough to leave any residue behind.

Look for any knots in the wood which seem to have
exuded resin. Such knots must be sealed with patent knotting to stop any bleeding later on. When dry, apply wood
primer. This seals the wood pores and provides a key for
the undercoat.

Follow with a putty filler if you have any cracks or holes
to fill. It should be applied after the primer so the oil in
the putty is not absorbed by the bare wood. If you prefer
to use a fine surface filler or a wood stopping, this should
be applied before the priming coat, and before the final
rub down.

With the primer dry, apply undercoat. Allow to dry, then
apply top coat, and a second top coat if possible.

Putty often presents problems in window frames, for it
hardens with age, and often falls out if the weather gets
behind it. In this respect, metal windows often are a bigger
problem than timber ones, for water vapour condenses
readily on metal frames, and the moisture from the glass
and the frame tries to get behind the putty. If it succeeds,
you get loose putty, very damp conditions, and perhaps
mould growths on the paintwork.

If putty is in a bad way, dig out loose pieces and brush
the frame clean. Timber frames should be sealed with
primer before new putty is applied, and metal frames
should be checked for rust before new metal casement putty
is applied. You need special putty for metal because of the
completely impervious nature of the frame.

When the putty has been replaced, clean off all dirt from the rest of the putty, then paint so that the paint goes about $\frac{1}{16}$ inch on to the glass, sealing that vital gap between glass and putty.

Now what if the glass is cracked or smashed? Remove all loose putty, then put on a pair of heavy leather gardening gloves and wiggle out the rest of the glass from the frame. Use an old stiff bladed knife, such as a cobbler's knife, to clear out all putty, and pull out any small nails you may find. When the frame is a metal one, you may find small glazing clips hooked into recesses in the frame. Note how they are fixed and remove them.

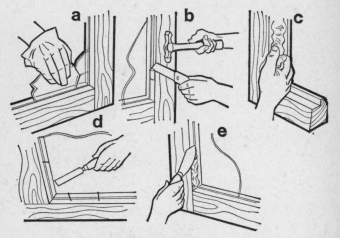

a, wear tough gloves. **b,** chip out old putty. **c,** feed new putty into rebate. **d,** tap in pins to hold glass. **e,** bevel off new putty

Brush the frame clean, then a timber one should be primed to stop suction. Now apply a bedding layer of putty along the inner rebate. The frame is now ready to take the new glass.

When measuring for glass, reduce the dimensions by $\frac{1}{8}$ inch each way, and check diagonals to see that the frame is square. If it is not, make a brown paper pattern of the exact shape. You can use the same method with odd shaped pieces such as you find in some front doors. Take your dimensions or your pattern to your glazier and let him cut it to size for you.

If you cut your own glass, choose a wheel cutter and a good straight-edge, and you need a little turps as a lubricant—and lots of practice on new glass. Don't try to cut down old glass. You are almost certain to crack it in the wrong places.

Place your new glass in the frame, and press it in from around the edges—never from the middle, or you will crack it. It should bed down on the layer of putty so that it squeezes out slightly underneath, thus cushioning the glass in the frame. Small glazing sprigs should be tapped into a timber frame to hold the glass while the putty sets. Replace the glazing clips in a metal frame (if any).

When putting in sprigs, slide a hammer or chisel over the glass into contact with the sprig so the glass never gets hit by a direct blow.

With the glass in place, apply the final layer of finishing putty, and use a putty knife to produce the correct angle. This is not easy, and like most things, practice makes perfect. A final dust over with a dry paint brush will smooth any wrinkles. Then leave the putty for about a week to surface-set before you paint.

When examining your frames, you may find cracks between brickwork and frame into which damp could get. This is usually caused by shrinkage of woodwork over the years, or the dropping out of any hard filling that had been applied. Clean out the gap as much as possible, then fill with a mastic filling compound. You can get this in tubes, and the filler is squeezed from the nozzle into the crack. The nozzle can be cut to give whatever width of flow is required. The mastic is very sticky, but it can be smoothed with a wet knife. This material sets surface-hard, but remains flexible

underneath, so it can remain sealed even with slight movement. The surface can be painted.

An alternative gap filler is a glazing cord. This is rather
like string covered in very sticky mastic, and it will effectively block cracks and keep the weather out.

Where a timber frame has been badly neglected, or where
poor quality timber was used in construction, you may find
part of the frame has been ruined by wet rot. The wood will
be crinkled and crumbly, and you can easily dig a knife
into it. In such cases the decayed wood must be cut out
right back to sound wood. Preservative should be applied,
then a new section of timber glued and pinned in place. Use
a waterproof glue for this job. Where rot is severe, the
frame will have to come out and be replaced.

Apart from actual structural faults, you may find that
timber frames go tight during winter months, then slacken
off during warmer weather. This is caused by expansion and
contraction of the timber, and you don't really solve the
problem by cutting strips from the frame. It is best to combine cutting a strip off with the application of a good
draught strip so that the actual sealing strip takes up any
variation of size.

Another cause of tightness is over-painting, so if a frame
is consistently tight, strip off the old paint down to bare
wood and re-paint.

This often happens with sash windows, when the recesses
in which the sashes run get clogged with paint coats.

Although some modern sash windows are spring controlled, most are counterbalanced by means of weights attached to cords. Cords can break, and if you have sashes
with broken cords, don't ignore them, for a falling sash can
easily break fingers. Many accidents are caused this way.
And if there is a cord to replace, you would be wise to replace all four at the same time, to save another session
fairly soon after. You have to take the sashes out anyway,
so it is not much extra work.

Buy only best quality waxed cord for this job. It is

usually sold in hanks of about 12 yards which should last quite a while.

With large windows you will need a bit of help lifting frames out. And don't attempt the job on a windy day.

First, lower the top sash (working from indoors) as far as it will go, then cut through the four cords as near the sashes as possible. Hold the cord and ease it over the pulley so the weight does not crash down.

Now ease away the two vertical beads, called the staff beads. An old chisel will do. Try not to damage these pieces of wood, as they have to go back. There are horizontal beads too, but there should be no need to remove these. Now you can swing out the lower sash and prise off the parting beads which will allow you to lift out the top sash.

With your old chisel, prise off the pocket pieces covering holes in the sash boxes. Feel inside and take out the two weights. You will also feel loosely secured dividing laths, and if you pull these to one side you can lift out the remaining two weights. Now remove all pieces of cut cord— from both weights and frames.

Now comes the re-cording operation. Tie a small weight to a length of thin string. The weight must be small enough to pass over the pulley wheels. Tie the other end of the string to one end of the new cord and pull the cord over pulley 1 in the drawing. Don't cut the cord, but feed it over pulley 2 in the same way, and pull it out of the box below. Now pass the weight and string over pulley 3, feed the cord down and out of the box below. Pass finally over pulley 4, feed down and out of the box below.

Remove the weight and string from the cord, and attach it to one of the weights just as it was originally fixed. If there is a slot for knots, make sure they are tucked well in so they don't interfere with the smooth running of the sash. Place the weight in the box below pulley 4, then pull on the cord where it passes over the pulley until the weight reaches the top of the box.

Now give a very firm pull to stretch the cord as much as

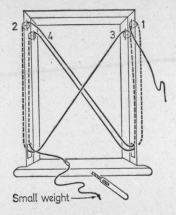

Small weight———➤

possible. Measure one quarter of the window height from
the bottom and cut the cord at this point, then anchor the
cord temporarily at this point with a staple. Some people
hammer a nail in the cord, but this can weaken it.

Tie the cut end of cord to another weight and place it
in the box below cord 3. Pull on this cord as before, cut
and secure. Repeat for pulleys 2 and 1.

Next release the cord connected with pulley 4 and attach
the cord to the left hand side of the upper sash, nailing it
firmly in the groove provided. Keep to the bottom of the
groove. Repeat with the cord over pulley 3. Place the frame
in its channel, replace the pocket pieces and parting beads
and test to see that the frame moves smoothly.

You will now have enough experience to repeat the process with the lower sash, making sure the cord is well
secured. Check for smooth running then replace the staff
beads.

Before you reassemble your sash window, it is a good
idea to check the pulley wheels for smooth running. This is
the time to oil them.

Doors

Most exterior doors are of softwood, but if kept well protected with paint they will give good service. Where a back door is exposed to wind and weather, even a simple porch will help protect it—and keep rain at bay.

Watch for signs of wet rot, particularly where paintwork has been neglected. You can recognise it by depressions in the wood, a wrinkled appearance, and a softness which allows a knife to be dug in quite easily. All damaged wood must be cut out, right back to sound wood, and new wood let in. If damage is bad, it is better to invest in a new door. Prices for such items are still reasonable.

Damaged glass can be replaced as for windows, except that a timber beading is usually used instead of a final layer of putty. The beading should be bedded on putty to seal the joint and to act as a buffer should the door slam.

If paint on a door is sound, it need only be washed down with sugar soap and flatted with a stripping block—as already mentioned for windows. Then new top coat can be applied—or an undercoat if there is a change of colour.

Slight damage from blisters or cracking can be locally repaired, but extensive flaking means the door needs stripping down and a new paint coating applied. Seal all knots with patent knotting, fill cracks and gaps with stopping or

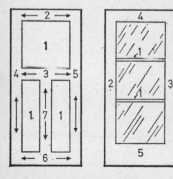

Paint doors in the order shown above

filler, then rub down, prime, rub lightly, undercoat, rub smooth and top coat. The order of working is shown in the illustration.

The same treatment applies to the door frames, and cracks between frame and wall can be sealed as mentioned for window frames.

Some better doors are made of oak, and very nice they can look until neglected. Where boiled linseed oil has been used to treat the wood, it eventually darkens and goes sticky. This must be completely stripped off with blowlamp and scraper, being very careful not to scorch the wood. If wax has been used on the door, buy a dewaxing compound and rub with this. It has a slight abrasive quality too, which helps to flat down the surface.

A power sander fitted with a fine abrasive pad is ideal for panels, but it should be either orbital in motion or in the form of a drum. This is so that no scratches are made across the wood grain. A disc sanding attachment should not be used, as this can score the wood.

A Skarsten scraper or a cabinet scraper, worked with the wood grain will offer a good alternative. Use glass paper in cracks and crevices, again always working with the wood grain. Where the wood has darkened, a wood bleach may help. Ask for details at your local paint stores and follow the directions very carefully.

To re-finish, use a polyurethane seal or an exterior grade varnish, and apply two or three coats. This will last far better than linseed oil.

Where doors are tight during winter and easy to open during dry weather, this is due to expansion and contraction of the wood. Ease off the door with a shaping tool or plane, going a little farther than necessary, then fix a good draught strip so that the strip takes up any variation in gap without letting in cold air. For durability, sprung plastic or bronze strip is better than foam plastic strip.

If a door is tight summer and winter, the cause may be

over-painting, or it may be slight sagging. If the latter is suspected, check that the hinges are really tight home. Slight extra recessing of one hinge or another may help pull the door away from the frame, but don't over-do this treatment or the door may not shut at all! The last resort is to plane off more door—which usually involves repainting.

Sometimes a door drops just a fraction in its frame so that lock and latch don't operate properly. The simplest remedy is to file a fraction off the bottom edge of the actual latch and mortise lock, and to round the edge very slightly. The two pieces will then usually go home easily with no further adjustment necessary.

5 Damp and Flooding

Before getting to grips with this chapter, read chapters 2 and 3 (if you have not already done so), for much mentioned there has a bearing on the subject of damp and how to deal with it.

One of the greatest problems in winter is that of damp. And the longer any gap in defences is neglected, the more damage is likely to be done. The best time to look for trouble is when it is pouring with rain—or has been raining continuously for some hours, for it is then that rain will search out weak spots.

Brick as weight

Starting at the very top of the house again, rain beating down a chimney may have little effect if the flue is in use, and continuously hot. But if that stack is no longer in use, the rain may settle on the internal lining, soak through, and appear in the house as damp—and often dirty—patches. If access is possible, a half tile can be set in mortar over the chimney pot. This will allow for ventilation, yet prevent the ingress of rain. Alternatively you can buy a proprietary capping pot which can in fact be lowered in place on the end of a long pole—ideal if you cannot get to the offending chimney easily. The cap is specially weighted so that it holds in place by gravity, and it has ventilation slots so that the chimney is not hermetically sealed.

Rain beating on to a porous chimney stack can have a considerable cooling effect, which in turn may upset the up-draught of a carefully controlled boiler. In the old days of inefficient boilers, considerable heat was lost up the chimney. Today, modern appliances can be set to slumber and there is very little pull up the flue. So, if these gases are cooled by a damp chimney, they may well condense on the flue lining in the form of a very corrosive liquid which, in time, will attack the flue lining and perhaps percolate through to an inner wall, making ugly stains on decorations. Treating the porous brickwork with a silicone water repellent, and re-pointing all damaged joints will help cure the trouble, but the ideal solution is to line the flue with a flexible flue lining or with salt glazed pipes, thus insulating the flue gases from the cold stack.

This treatment is best carried out by a professional—and if you do plan to have the job done, there is another alternative—that of calling in a company to line the flue with a special insulating material, leaving a hole for gases up the centre. This is achieved by lowering an inflated tube into the flue; pouring in a special lightweight concrete, then withdrawing the tube.

If rain penetrates the flashing around a chimney stack, it will either flow down the actual stack into the loft, and perhaps down into a bedroom, or it may be diverted down one of the roof rafters, to appear as a damp patch on a ceiling quite a distance from the root of the trouble. That is why a search in the rain helps, for you can often actually see the path of the water; whereas when the rain stops, there may be no indication at all as to where the damp originated.

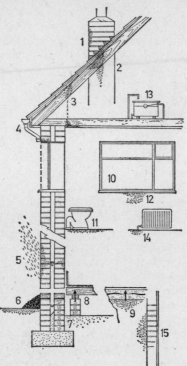

1. Damaged chimney flaunching, brickwork or pointing
2. Loose or damaged flashing
3. Damaged, loose or missing slates or tiles
4. Defective guttering and downpipes
5. Porous brickwork and pointing; bridged wall ties
6. Bridged damp proof course
7. Defective d.p.c. sleeper wall
9. Damaged or non-existent d.p.c. in a solid floor
10. Condensation on windows
11. Condensation on toilet pans and cisterns
12. Damp patches on walls
13. Leaks in plumbing
14. Leaks in central heating
15. Damp in basement

The same applies to displaced or damaged slates and tiles. Water entering may trickle down a rafter for a considerable distance before dripping off on to a ceiling. There it will form a pool, gather dirt and eventually soak through to form a dirty mark on the ceiling.

An overflowing gutter may well attract attention by the dramatic waterfall flowing past a window, but keep an eye open too for the more dangerous overflow which finds its way via a gutter bracket on to the house wall. This concentration of water will find any weak spot in the wall, and you can soon have damp patches indoors, ruining decorations.

Check very carefully for cracks or gaps in gutters— especially where one section joins another, and where the gutter joins the down pipe. And see that gutters and pipes are free from obstruction.

Porous walls and faulty d.p.c.s are dealt with in detail in chapter 3, but do bear in mind that treatment is best carried out in dry weather when the walls are free to absorb the preventive liquid applied. Obviously, a silicone water repellent applied to a soaking wet wall can give only very superficial treatment.

While brickwork and other masonry may not suffer much from continuous damp, timber in contact with the damp will soon be seriously affected unless very well protected. It must always be remembered that once timber is cut, and is therefore no longer living, it is nature's way to reduce it to basic elements. This can be seen happening in any wood or forest, thus ensuring that living timber is not impeded by dead wood. And, unfortunately, nature does not discriminate between a log in the forest and a window frame in your house!

In constantly damp conditions, where the wood has a moisture content above 30 per cent, wet rot fungus takes over. It is recognisable by its blackish strands, and by the way it soon robs timber of its strength. Cracks appear, mainly along the grain. The wood structure collapses, and a knife can be easily dug into the wood, and the wood prised away.

Fortunately wet rot is confined to the damp wood. It does not spread outside that area. All damaged wood must be cut away until completely sound timber is encountered, then new wood, preferably pre-treated with a good preservative, should be inserted. You can buy from many good timber merchants special pre-treated timber which has been pressure impregnated. It is well worth the little extra expense

to get such timber, for it will be highly resistant to all forms of attack.

Far more dangerous and damaging is the dry rot fungus. Where water content of timber exceeds 20 per cent, coupled with very poor or non-existent ventilation, the spores of the dry rot fungus take root. A fruiting body grows, from which whitish strands spread rapidly, feeding on the cellulose in the timber. Once the rot gets a grip, the wood loses all strength; it cracks across and with the grain, and a knife point can easily be pushed into the wood.

The attack is associated with a most unpleasant musty smell, coupled with warped woodwork and a latticework of whitish strands, and it is often found under floors—especially where ventilation has been blocked.

The biggest problem is that once the rot gets a hold, it is

able to feed water along its strands to make damp dry areas of timber. It can pass through brick walls and travel considerable distances, and it has been known to start in a house cellar and appear in the loft!

As soon as you suspect an attack of dry rot, take action. Eradication is best left to experts because of the serious nature of the rot, and you will find in your telephone book the addresses of companies who will offer a free survey, plus advice on what treatment is required. Every bit of damaged wood must come out and be burned; masonry must be treated with powerful fungicides, and often heated with a blowlamp to sterilise it. And the rot must be traced to its farthest point, otherwise the attack will quickly get underway again.

New timber installed should be pre-treated against attack, then steps must be taken to eradicate all traces of damp, and to improve ventilation. Good ventilation is vital.

Waterlogged ground can be a very real problem in areas where clay predominates. If ground slopes away, water may drain through the top soil and away, but wherever there are hollows or perhaps shallow valleys, water will gather on top of the clay. If a home is sited at the bottom of the hollow, the water may well force its way into basements or ground floors.

If you meet such a situation, it may be possible for land drains to be inserted into the ground to collect and divert water. The drains are made of porous or holed pipes fitted loosely together, and the pipes are led away to a suitable drainage area or ditch. Of course, siting of such pipes is a skilled job, so it would be as well to call in your borough surveyor to advise. Whether or not you can actually put in the pipes will depend upon the depth they must go and the length of run. In most cases it is a job best left to the expert and his ditch-digging machinery.

Where a house is situated in an area subject to flooding after severe rainfall, there is not a lot one can do to avoid trouble. Where water is likely to be shallow, and where it recedes quickly, it pays at all costs to keep water out of air bricks which lead to the foundations. If you can seal them over in time with a mastic sealing tape held in place by a sheet of light gauge metal, in turn held by clips or screws, this will help. But it is a matter of being prepared.

What so often happens is that water enters the air bricks, fills the underfloor cavity, then water enters the house through the floor, with disastrous results. If you can block the air bricks and cracks below doors, there is a chance you will reduce entry to a minimum.

If you have solid ground floors, the above will not of course apply as there will be no cavity below.

When laying out gardens you know are likely to flood, do keep this in mind, and make sure that water would have a free flow away. I recall one garden where a flooded road allowed water to pour in through the drive gates of a house towards the house, but a garden path swung round and out of the front gate which, due to a slight drop in level, encouraged the water to follow! The house remained unaffected by the torrent.

Be prepared also for water to back up drains and come out of manholes and gulleys. You cannot hold a manhole down which is under pressure—even with the weight of a car. Don't be tempted to lower those little raised walls around gulleys adjoining your house. If water does back up the drains, these walls will retain the water. If you lower the walls, water may flow out and cause extra flooding.

What should you do if, despite precautions, you are flooded? Of course there will be salvage work to do on possessions, but we will concentrate here on the actual house fabric.

The first job is to hose everywhere down and put down disinfectant. So often water is forced up from the sewers, bringing a very unhealthy sludge with it. Lift manholes and sluice these down too. See they are not blocked by debris, and that water is flowing freely from the house drains.

With timber floors, lift boards and examine the foundations. In severe cases the local authorities will bring in pumps to drain off trapped water, then use powerful industrial blowers to start drying out.

It is essential to keep air moving. That means leaving up floorboards, applying fan heaters to damp areas and perhaps taking out extra bricks at ventilation brick level to increase the flow of air. With plenty of air on the move, the chances of dry rot are slight, but if you shut the damp areas off too soon, you could be in trouble.

Watch out for mould growth too. There are always spores in the air, and they breed in damp conditions, appearing as coloured spots or greenish patches, according to type. Treat all mould with a fungicide. If the mould appears on wallpaper, this must be ripped off and the plaster below treated.

Don't be in a hurry to redecorate. You really need spring drying winds—and perhaps summer too, before the fabric is really dry. Papering too early may well involve more mould.

You will find more about treating walls in chapter 7.

6 The House Surrounds

However carefully you paint and decorate the outside of the house, the over-all effect will be made or marred by the condition of the surrounds. That is the paths and drives, gates and fences.

First, the concrete work. Paths in poor shape very quickly deteriorate once winter frosts get a grip. Water freezing in cracks and gaps expands, further breaking down the surface. Providing the base is sound, you may be able to re-surface the path with a thin layer of new material. But do bear in mind that you must not bring the path up closer than 6 inches to the damp proof course level. Until quite recently re-surfacing was not really practical unless the new layer was really thick, but with the introduction of a new adhesive known as pva, it is possible to feather down new concrete on old to as little as $\frac{1}{8}$ inch.

The pva is bought by the can from builders' merchants, and is added to the water which will be added to the concrete. Be guided by the instructions on the can as to the amount to be added. Once added, providing the old concrete is clear of loose material and is not coated with oil or grease, the concrete will adhere firmly to the old path. It also helps to brush a coating on the old path prior to placing new concrete. This will increase adhesion. Another advantage of a pva mix is that is eliminates dusting of concrete—a menace on many garage floors.

As an alternative to laying new concrete, the old path can be covered with a cold asphalt. This is bought by the paper sack from many builders' merchants and garden suppliers. Some need a primer; some don't.

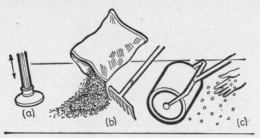

Remove all loose and flaking material from the old path, then prime if necessary with the liquid emulsion supplied for the job. Now tip the cold asphalt out and rake it level to the thickness recommended by the maker. Wet the drum of a fairly heavy garden roller to prevent the metal sticking to the asphalt. Roll well, and before the final rolling, add the contrasting chippings to give a speckled effect. Don't over-do the chippings or you end up with an 'aftermath of the wedding' effect—which just looks a mess.

Cold asphalt can also be used on ground which has been well consolidated and strengthened with rubble, but it should never be used on just bare earth.

Often work may involve extending a path, or putting one where none exists. This is not a difficult job, but it does involve quite a bit of preparatory work.

First, clear all topsoil from the path area to a depth of about 3 inches, then ram in rubble, and work it level, bearing in mind that you want a minimum depth of 3 inches of concrete. You then need lengths of timber which will give you the required 3 inches depth. Lay these on the boundary of the path, and knock in pegs to the outside of the timber to keep the timber in place when concrete is poured. Use a string line to help get path runs true.

The path is best divided into bays about 8ft. long to allow for ground movement. You can either put thin softwood laths across at 8ft. centres and leave them in, or you can put temporary lengths of wood across, fill alternate

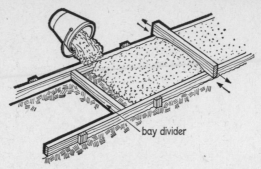

bay divider

bays, then remove the wood strips. Either method is accept-able.

When concrete has been tipped in a bay, it should be levelled with a length of wood which has a concave shape on the underside. This will give the path a slight convex surface which will help shed rainwater.

With the path finished, cover the area with damp sacking or with polythene sheeting to retain the moisture in the setting concrete. If the concrete dries off too quickly it will be weak and brittle.

Where paths come against the house, instead of a convex surface, give the path a fall away from the house. A fall of about 1 inch every 6 feet is suitable, and this should be set at the setting out stage using a spirit level.

Having laid out your path, you can gauge what volume of concrete is required. Work out the area of the path in square feet, then multiply by the thickness—in this case 3 inches—then divide the answer by 12. The answer is the number of cubic feet of concrete required. To recap: Area in square feet × thickness in inches divided by 12 = cubic feet required.

You now have a choice of ways of tackling the problem.

First, you can order ready-mixed concrete from one of the many firms who offer this service. They prefer to deliver 3 to 6 cubic yards, but most will supply as little as one

cubic yard for an extra delivery charge. You must explain
what job you have in mind so they can supply the right
mix, and if possible, you should arrange access near the
site. Clearance between gate posts must be at least 9 feet and
the drive needs to be at least 4in. thick if it is to take the
weight of the lorry without damaging the concrete.

If this is not possible, arrange for a chain of three or
four barrows, plus helpers, and a gangway of planks. You
have not a lot of time to play with once the water is added
to the mix—especially in warm weather!

Second, you can hire a cement mixer; buy the necessary
materials and mix your own concrete on site. This takes the
real backache out of the job, but adds a hire charge to your
expenses.

Third, if only a very small area is to be repaired, you can
buy dry concrete mixes from most builders' merchants which
only need the addition of water. The cost of buying this
way is much higher when bulk is concerned, but for small
jobs it pays off—and there is the convenience of being able
to stack supplies neatly on site. Very important where space
is limited.

Now a word about ingredients.

Cement is supplied in paper sacks containing about 1cwt.,
and it is normally grey in colour. If you want a different
colour, you can buy special dry pigments which are added
to the mix before adding water. Cement should always be
fresh and dry.

Sand comes in two main types—sharp and builders'. The
sharp sand is very gritty like the sand on the sea shore and
is used in concreting. Builders' sand is soft and relatively
smooth, and this is used for mortar. Whichever type you
have to use, it must be clean—and that means free from
clay and dirt.

Aggregate comes in two main types, but you can get
general mix or all-in ballast where uniformity in the concrete is not important. Coarse aggregate can be gravel or
crushed stone between $\frac{3}{4}$ inch and $\frac{3}{16}$ inch, and this is fine

for general work. But where concrete will be less than 2 inches thick use fine aggregate with particles not more than $\frac{3}{8}$ inch.

Mixes

Where you want a strong concrete with resistance to wear, use a 1 cement, 2 sand, 3 coarse aggregate by volume mix— and keep water down to a minimum. This will be suitable for paths, pools, steps and any fairly thick section work on path repairs. As the volume of mixed concrete is always less than the total volume of mixed ingredients you must take this into consideration. As a guide : 1 bag of cement, $2\frac{1}{2}$ cubic feet of sand and $3\frac{3}{4}$ cubic feet of coarse aggregate will produce $\frac{1}{5}$ cubic yard of mix. Where a lower grade of concrete will suffice, use 1 part cement, $2\frac{1}{2}$ sand and 4 coarse aggregate by volume. This will be suitable for foundation work, garage floors, drives and thick walls.

In this case, 1 bag of cement, $3\frac{1}{8}$ cubic feet of sand and 5 cubic feet of coarse aggregate will yield about $\frac{1}{4}$ cubic yard of mix.

Where thin sections are involved, such as path repairs, use a 1 cement, 3 sharp sand by volume mix. This can also be used for making paving slabs less than 2 inches thick. With builders' sand substituted for the sharp sand, this is the mix for mortar. Here, 1 bag of cement and $3\frac{3}{4}$ cubic feet of sand will yield about $\frac{1}{7}$ cubic yard of mortar.

For bedding paving slabs to a firm base, use a 1 cement to 5 sand by volume mix. One bag of cement and $6\frac{1}{4}$ cubic feet of sand will yield about $\frac{1}{6}$ cubic yard of mortar.

In all cases keep the water down to a minimum. Too much will weaken the mix and cause shrinkage when it hardens. You should just be able to mould it so that it holds a shape without slumping.

The secret of mixing is to get a completely uniform colour throughout before adding water. And don't mix more than you can use within an hour. Take care to wash down all items used before concrete dries on them, but should you get a build-up on tools and plant—or spills on brickwork—you can buy special liquids which dissolve the concrete without harming other materials. Use strictly to the instructions.

Where you just wish to repair cracks and gaps, use a 1 cement 3 sand mix with the addition of pva adhesive. Be sure to rake out all loose material and break off any crumbling pieces, then damp the cracks with water so you get no suction of water from the new concrete. Press well into the cracks with a trowel, then level off. Don't trowel over it too much or you will draw cement to the surface.

When the concrete starts to set, you can brush over the surface with a stiffish brush so the surface is not too smooth. The same treatment can be given to larger areas of new concrete to make it non-slip. If you want a really textured surface, you can continue brushing until the stones in the mix stand proud.

Don't neglect damaged steps. Frost can attack brick supports, causing them to flake away, and it can also cause pieces of step to break off. Deal with damage as soon as possible, before someone has an accident. Very often, worn or damaged paving slabs can be lifted and turned over to present a new face, or they can be turned around so that a damaged edge is put to the back. A 1 cement to 5 sand mix

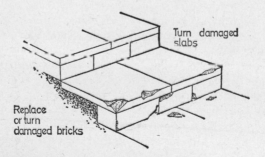

Turn damaged slabs

Replace or turn damaged bricks

can be used to bed-in the slabs. Again damp the slabs to
stop suction.

Very often, paved areas develop slopes, or odd slabs rock
when you tread on them. This is caused by settlement under
the slab, very often attributed to poor foundations. Lift
any offending slabs, remove the old mortar, put down a bit
of rubble and ram it well into the ground. Then put down
five blobs of new mortar (one at each corner and a largish
one at the centre) and tamp down the slab, having first
wet the underside. Use the handle of a club hammer or a
rubber mallet, and tap lightly but firmly. Don't use a metal
implement, which could crack the slab.

Should a slab be cracked in two, use the technique as
above, with plenty of new mortar at the centre to support
the broken pieces.

Remember with all concrete work to damp the drying
surface if the weather is very dry, and to keep the surface
well covered with damp sacking or polythene sheeting to
retard drying out.

Paths and patios can be tackled by buying ready-made
slabs, ranging from second-hand paving slabs sold by your
local council to textured, coloured units available in a range
of sizes from specialist firms. Many firms supply a squared
leaflet upon which you can mark the area you have to cover,
and any chosen pattern or colour combination. By colour-
ing in and marking the squares, this will help you decide
how many slabs you need of any size or colour. If this
seems too hard, many firms will help you if you give them
details of area and slab choice.

Slabs may be laid on a sand base, where the sand is laid
on rammed hardcore; on a bed of mortar, or on five spots
of mortar, as already mentioned. Dry-laying on sand is the
method least likely to stand up to settlement or heavy wear.

Drives can be repaired as mentioned for paths, and here
you may find cracking more severe if inadequate founda-

tions were laid initially. A drive must be based on a good surface of rammed rubble, followed by a minimum of 4 inches of top concrete. Be very wary of allowing a ready-mixed concrete lorry to back up your drive, especially during damp weather. The very heavy load could prove too much for your concrete.

7 Interior Walls

As mentioned earlier in this book, modern wall construction may vary quite a bit, but it is fair to say that most homes have plaster on brick for the outer walls. If yours is a between-the-wars house, you probably have cavity walls, the inner leaf of each wall finished with plaster, with a skim coat of fine plaster to give a good smooth finish. Most post-war houses are of similar construction, but breeze or other lightweight block may be used for the inner wall leaf instead of brick.

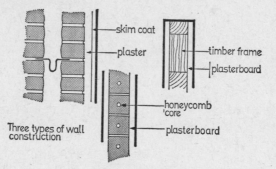

skim coat

plaster

timber frame

plasterboard

honeycomb 'core

plasterboard

Three types of wall construction

Dividing walls within the house can vary quite a bit. They may be plastered brick, plastered block, timber and plasterboard partition, or special hollow plasterboard. The governing factor in most homes is whether the dividing walls are loadbearing or not. Loadbearing walls are those actually supporting upper floors, so they are built sturdily on foundations. Non-load-bearing walls are those which have been added after the house has been built, merely to divide up living areas—and as such, they don't need to be so robust. It will pay you to find out just which walls do what in your own home—especially if you have future plans for demolishing walls to make two rooms into one large one.

Outer walls are the ones which give most problems, and of those, ones facing north, and house corners, are the worst, for these get coldest and are thus most prone to damp. Most troubles will be associated with points brought out in chapter 3, so keep an eye on that chapter as you study this one.

Damp is the greatest spoiler of wall plaster and decorations, and when discovered, it should be dealt with as quickly as possible. Let us examine some causes. (See page 46.)

Defective guttering may allow water to soak into a wall adjoining it, and this water may find a route across to the inner plaster just below ceiling level. The plaster will become saturated, appearing as damp patches on wallpaper, perhaps with mould growth. First, the gutter trouble must be put right, then the wall allowed to dry out. This is not so easy in the winter, so drying can be speeded up by placing a fan heater near the wall to create a flow of warm air.

If mould is encountered, the plaster must be treated with a fungicide to kill all spores. If you don't, new fungus stains may well appear on any new decoration.

Porous outer brickwork combined with heavy rain, plus bridged wall ties, may also result in damp patches. Here, treatment of the outer wall as suggested in chapter 3 is the first step, followed by a good drying out period. Treat fungus mould as above.

Condensation is a real modern menace in the home—especially with the growth of full central heating. In our old, draughty houses with their open fires, large quantitites of air were always on the move, and moisture was ejected. Today, with our fireplaces blocked up; full central heating, and all cracks and crevices sealed, moisture produced stays in the house, often with destructive results.

What exactly is condensation? And how can we distinguish it from damp coming through from outside? Warm air in a home is able to absorb a considerable amount of moisture vapour produced by cooking, bathing, washing—and even breathing. And there the vapour stays until any colder surface is encountered. As soon as air is cooled, its ability to hold water vapour is reduced, and some of the vapour is deposited in the form of minute droplets we call condensation.

It is recognisable as condensation because you see it on cold, crisp, dry days. Other damp may be seen on damp, mild, rainy days. As a second check, if damp patches appear at times when windows are steamed up, suspect condensation, for windows present probably the most vulnerable surface for the deposit of moisture vapour.

Condensation will form on outer walls, these being far colder than inner dividing walls. And it will usually pick the very coldest spots on walls, such as house corners or walls exposed to cold winds. It will also form where air is still, such as behind wardrobes and other pieces of furniture. The end result will be damp patches ruining decorations; a musty, dank smell, and probably mould growth.

What can be done to combat it? Moisture extraction is of prime importance, preferably at or near source. In other words, fit an extractor fan in the kitchen, and a small one in the bathroom. Cooker hoods are fine for the extraction of cooking smells and steam, but they don't deal with other steam-producing equipment probably sited in the kitchen as well. So, it probably pays to fit a fan in a wall or window large enough to deal with the whole kitchen.

Keep doors shut when washing, bathing or cooking, otherwise the damp air passes to the rest of the house, circulating until it finds a cold room, where moisture will condense. This accounts for the surprise some people express when damp patches appear in a room not even in use. When

filling a bath, run a little cold in first, then feed hot under
the cold from a length of hose. In this way steam is kept to
a minimum.

Warming cold wall surfaces will also help. A tubular
heater placed at the base of a cold wall area will produce
sufficient heat to keep the wall dry. Such heaters are only
rated at 60 watts per foot, so they are quite economical to
operate even over long periods.

Also, pull furniture just a little away from cold walls to
allow air to circulate behind.

Yet another approach is to cover the wall in a veneer of
insulation such as expanded polystyrene. This is stuck to
the wall with a special adhesive, and, once on, it can be
papered over. Or you can have the wall cavities filled with
a special insulating foam which sets after insertion. This
is an excellent insulator.

It should be borne in mind that such a covering will not
stop damp striking through a wall. In fact such damp will
push the insulation off the wall—and any wallpaper with
it.

Damp may also strike up from the foundations if a damp
proof course is faulty or non-existent. Here, damp patches
appear at just above skirting level, usually during damp
weather. Again, the trouble must be dealt with, and a sound
d.p.c. inserted, or one of the remedies suggested in chapter 5.

A whole range of special damp resisting membranes are
produced for sticking to internal walls to hold back damp.
Their use should be very carefully considered. While they
may hide the damp from one room, remember the damp
still exists in the wall, and it may climb higher in an attempt to find a way out. So, trouble which started in a
lounge may well appear as damp patches in a bedroom
above. It always pays to locate the actual cause of the
damp, and eliminate it at source.

If damp is discovered at skirting board level, examine

the skirting board for possible rotting. Damp rot is most common, and if this is discovered, the board must be cut out and replaced.

Usually it is fairly easy to prise away a skirting board from the plugs to which it is nailed. The most difficult part is getting new skirting to match, for there are very many types and sizes. If you take a piece to your timber merchant, he will be able to match it—for a price. Or you can buy prepared timber as near as possible in size, then shape it yourself. I have done this using a power tool and a tungsten carbide abrasive disc, finishing off with a drum sander —and saving a lot of money in the process.

If there is a chance of future damp, be sure to treat the timber with preservative. Or, you can buy special fungicidal plugs. These are inserted into the wall, where they remain until damp touches them. Then, part of the plug dissolves spreading a powerful fungicide which kills off any fungus spores and protects the wood. It will pay also to check floors for signs of rot. See chapter 8.

Apart from spoiling decoration, damp will soften plaster, eventually reducing it to a crumbling mass. Drying it out will not improve matters, so all crumbling plaster must be cut away and new plaster inserted.

While dealing with damaged plaster, keep an eye open for small patches of condensation forming on an otherwise unaffected wall. This is a common fault in older property, and

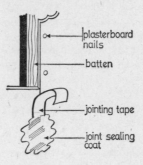

plasterboard nails

batten

jointing tape

joint sealing coat

the cause is areas of dense plaster, probably applied as war damage repairs, which are unable to absorb any moisture. If you strip off the paper or paint from a wall, you will usually see them as areas of different coloured plaster. Hack them out and replace with a less dense mix. Make sure you get the surface dead smooth with the surrounding area, or if you fit wall lights, shadows may be thrown where the different levels meet.

Where a wall is really bad, it may be easier to cut off all the old plaster and re-cover the wall with sheet plasterboard. This may either be nailed to battens pinned to the wall, or stuck direct to the wall with a special adhesive. There is an art in sealing the gaps between boards, and if you want to tackle this job, you would be wise to get a book of instructions from one of the large gypsum wallboard companies. This will explain what materials are needed, and how the job is done, step by step. The addition of a layer of plasterboard also is an effective way of insulating a very cold wall surface.

Chimney breast walls can also give trouble if damp has entered the actual flue. Chemical deposits on the flue lining may be carried through the wall by moisture to appear as very nasty stains on decorations and plaster. Here too the damp must be dealt with, then the stain sealed off. This can be done by means of one of the sheet membranes designed for wall sealing, or by sealing the wall with an aluminium sealer. This is a special aluminium paint of scale-like nature which effectively seals off a surface. Ordinary primer made of ground aluminium is not suitable.

Basements and other rooms where a wall is backed on the far side by soil has particular problems. If damp-resisting liquids fail, the wall is best covered with a special material called *Newtonite* lath. This is a special damp-proof corrugated sheeting supplied in rolls. Once fixed, it may be plastered over to form a new wall surface. If you plan to use this material, get an instruction book or leaflet from your local stockists so that you know exactly how to

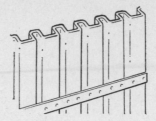

apply it. Again, remember such a material effectively holds back damp. It does not cure it.

Apart from damp, very little affects wall plaster. House settlement may cause cracking, or general drying out of plaster may cause fine cracks. Really fine crazing can be ignored if the wall is to be papered, but if you wish to paint, rub over the wall with a coarse rag dipped in cellulose filler. Allow to dry, then rub smooth with glasspaper.

Larger cracks should be raked out to remove all crumbling material, and slight undercutting of the crack will help key the repair material to the wall—even though manufacturers of certain proprietary materials say this is not necessary. Apply cellulose filler with a small trowel just proud of the surface, allow to dry, then rub smooth. It is wise to damp cracks before filling so that moisture is not drawn from the filler, weakening it.

Where cracks are large, or where pieces of plaster have dropped out, a cellulose filler can work out expensive. In this case a material such as Keenes cement is perfectly satisfactory, and it costs a lot less. Again, fill just proud of the wall surface, then rub smooth.

Decorating Walls

Assuming that walls are in good condition, there are many ways they can be decorated ranging from a coat of paint to an expensive panelling. Choose wisely, and bear in mind that often your choice will be with you for many years That coat of paint will never come off again—and panelling is too expensive for most of us to discard after a few years. Let us look at some decorations in more detail.

Painting Walls

Modern emulsion coatings have made the painting of walls very popular, and the big advantage is that if you tire of a colour, it is only the work of a few hours to put on a new coat. Modern pigments are such that in many cases only one new coat is necessary to obliterate an under-colour, but where drastic changes are required, it pays to experiment.

Emulsion paint can be applied over old wallpaper providing the paper is clean and grease-free, and that the paper is adhering well to the wall. Again, if there is any doubt, experiment, for in some cases the water content of the new paint loosens weak adhesive and the paper may blister and pull off the wall. Even vinyl wallcoverings in good condition can be painted with vinyl emulsion—as long as the texture doesn't offend.

To apply paint, use a mohair or foam plastic roller, spreading the paint in all directions—not working to set lines. A very good alternative—and my favourite—is to use one of the larger painting pads. These consist of a pad of mohair bonded to a pad of foam, which in turn is fixed to a plastic or metal handle. Again, paint is put on working in all directions, and you will find there is no spatter or dripping as you get with some paint rollers.

If you choose to use a brush, make sure it is 5 inches or 6 inches wide, or you will find it takes a long time to cover an area, and the edges will dry off. It is wise to keep a 1 inch or $1\frac{1}{2}$ inch brush handy for finishing corners and edges.

Remember that once you have painted over wallpaper, it is going to be very hard to get it off. If you have to face this job, first go over the surface with an open coat abrasive disc or with a wire brush to cut through the paint coat. Then add a little cellulose paste and liquid detergent to warm water and wet the wall. The paste helps hold water in place, while the detergent acts as a wetting agent. As an alternative, if you don't mind a little extra outlay, hire a steam wallpaper stripper, and this will take off paint and paper without wire brushing.

Emulsion paint can be applied to bare plaster, in which case it is best to dilute a quantity of paint with an equal quantity of water and use this as a primer. Follow this with a full coat. Don't rely on paint to fill even minor cracks. It won't. Either fill all cracks, or apply a lining paper to the wall then paint over it. The big advantage of the latter is that should you wish to strip to bare plaster, you can get the lining paper off. My experience is that once bare plaster is painted, it is as good as impossible to strip it clean.

A tip about buying paint: be sure to buy enough in one go, as batches may vary slightly in colour. Far better buy a gallon than eight one pint tins if you want to be sure of a good over-all colour.

I can think of no case where it is wise to use an oil-based paint on a wall. The high gloss shows up every blemish; it is not cheap, and you can't get it off. Apart from this, it clogs the pores of the plaster, making condensation far more likely. If you want a glazed surface for cleanliness, it is better to spend a little extra and use tiles.

Plain brickwork indoors can be emulsion coated, but be warned it looks just like painted brickwork! And you will never get the paint off. In really olde worlde period homes, this effect can look quite attractive, but in more modern property it would probably pay to line the wall with plaster-board then decorate over this.

Where walls are rather uneven yet you wish to paint, first cover the walls with a heavily embossed *Anaglypta* paper. This heavy paper is available in a number of interesting designs ranging from imitation plaster daub to basket weave. It is applied with a fairly heavy paste, and you must remember not to press down the edges where the raised pattern is. The bumps on one length should mate with the bumps on the next. If you press the pattern down, you will see a vertical line of smooth paper down each seam.

Yet another textured material, with even more relief, is the architectural panel, now available through many decorators shops. It comes in a variety of effects, from pebbles to futuristic designs, and the panels are stuck in place with a special adhesive. If you paint these, some can be tackled with along pile lambswool roller, but for safety, a wide brush is probably best. Take care not to press the relief in.

Lincrusta is also a relief decorative material. It rather resembles putty moulded on paper, and designs include imitation rope pattern, wood grain effects and simulated planking or panelling. Again, a special adhesive is required.

Wallpapering

By far the most popular way of decorating walls is to use wallpaper, even though it is a rather tedious process compared with painting. Patterns today are endless, offering a variety of delightful effects and colours. And you will find weights of paper vary too, often according to price. It is impossible to tell what a pattern or colour will really look like from the piece you see in the pattern book, so try to see a roll opened out. You may then find the colour overpowering, or the flowers far too large for the room you have in mind. And for your first attempt, try to use a random pattern that does not need careful matching. That will be one worry less! Don't choose a very cheap paper assuming you will be saving money. The paper is usually so thin that it rips too easily when pushed about. Go for a medium-weight paper which can take a bit of rough handling.

The first important job is to get the walls prepared. Old wallpaper should be removed by soaking well with water. It helps to add a little detergent and some cellulose paste to the water. Leave to soak, then strip off the paper with a scraper, taking care not to damage the plaster. Where obstinate, heavy, papers are encountered, it may pay you to hire a wallpaper stripping machine for a day. This produces steam and conveys it to a metal plate specially perforated

to allow the steam to hit the wallpaper. In a matter of
seconds, even a thick paper will drop away. Take care when
working near the ceiling, for you can easily loosen ceiling
paper too!

It is possible to paper over existing paper if it is clean
and grease-free, but I don't think it is good practice. Also
you must test to see that the old paper is adhering well,
otherwise the new paper may pull the old from the wall as
the water from the new paste soaks in.

Emulsion-covered walls should be washed down, then
roughened with coarse glasspaper. Gloss paint should be
similarly treated, but do make sure the gloss is broken down
as much as possible.

Distempered walls should be carefully examined. Water-
bound distemper must be washed off with a coarse rag. If
this is not possible, the distemper must be stabilised with
a special distemper sealer. Washable distemper should be
washed down, then the wall scoured with coarse glasspaper.

With the wall cleaned down, fill all cracks and holes with
a proprietary filler. Work just proud of the surface, then
when the filler is hard, smooth over with fine glasspaper.

Now you need to get your materials together, and a list is
strongly advised.

Order enough paper—or a little over. Most shops will
take back an unopened roll, but they may have difficulty
in getting one more roll from the same batch. If they cannot,
colours may be very slightly different. The chart will give a
guide to the number of rolls required. When ordering, check
on the distance between pattern repeats. For a large repeat
you may need to allow more for wastage than for, say, an
over-all design with no repeat.

Many papers and vinyls now come pre-pasted, but here
we will stick to the basic traditional methods. Just about
all coverings are pre-trimmed.

WALLS

Measurement in feet round walls, including Doors and Windows

Height in feet from skirting	28	32	36	40	44	48	52	56	60	64	68	72	76	80	84	88	92	96	100
7 and under 7½	4	4	5	5	6	6	7	7	8	8	9	9	9	10	10	11	11	12	12
7½ and under 8	4	4	5	5	6	6	7	8	8	9	9	10	10	11	11	12	12	13	13
8 and under 8½	4	5	5	6	6	7	7	8	8	9	9	10	10	11	12	13	13	13	14
8½ and under 9	4	5	5	6	6	7	8	8	9	9	10	11	11	12	12	13	13	14	14
9 and under 9½	4	5	6	6	7	7	8	9	9	10	10	11	12	12	13	13	14	15	15
9½ and under 10	5	5	6	7	7	8	9	9	10	10	11	12	12	13	14	14	15	15	16
10 and under 10½	5	5	6	7	8	8	9	10	10	11	12	12	13	14	14	15	16	16	17
10½ and under 11	5	6	7	7	8	9	9	10	11	11	12	13	13	14	15	16	16	17	18
11 and under 11½	5	6	7	8	8	9	10	10	11	12	13	13	14	15	16	16	17	18	18

There are two main types of paste from which to choose, the cellulose paste and the heavier starch paste. Cellulose paste is practically transparent and thus shows up less on the surface of a paper, but it does have a higher water content. Starch paste has far more solids and less water, so while it tends to show on the surface of a paper, it does grip it more firmly.

Walls should be sized before papering to seal the surface and to ensure good paper 'slip'. If you choose a cellulose paste, this is used also as size. If you choose a full bodied starch paste, you need to buy a packet of glue size. The glue size is dissolved in boiling water, and is best applied to the wall with a wide brush. Put plenty of newspaper down as it tends to splash.

For actual tools you need at least one scraper (already mentioned for stripping), stepladder, folding wood rule or steel tape, chalk and plumbline, paperhanger's scissors, paste brush, paperhanging brush to smooth paper on wall, bucket for clean water, and clean rags for wiping down, and a pasting table at least 2 feet wide. My pasting table is an old painted door, kept in the garage, rested on two stools—but you can buy proper tables for a reasonable price if you prefer it. Finally, you need a pencil.

When mixing the paste, its thickness should be governed by the weight of paper being hung. Thin paper, thin paste; heavy paper, thick paste. And soaking time will depend on paper thickness as well. The heavier papers, and especially embossed ones, should be allowed to soak after pasting for five minutes or so to allow the paper to expand. Once you get into the swing, it may be possible to paste a second length while the first is soaking.

Failure to let the paper expand results in continued expansion on the wall, and you get blisters. Don't assume these will shrink back as the paper dries out. They rarely do.

Having got to this point, just a reminder that any paintwork which butts against paper is best painted prior to papering while the walls are stripped. At door frames, skirtings and picture rails, take your paint on to the wall just a fraction so that if your paper should fall a little short, you won't see bare plaster.

Now back to papering. Where do you start? The best place is in the corner marked A on the diagram, and work away from the light. This is so that should you even slightly overlap one piece of paper over another, no shadow will be thrown by light from the window.

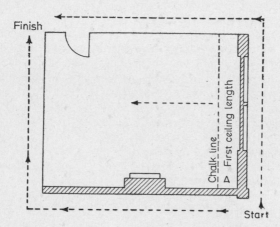

Assuming your paper width is 20¾ inches (but it may vary) rub your plumb line with coloured chalk; measure 19¾ inches from the corner; make a pencil mark, then hang the plumb line on the mark. When it settles, snap the line to leave a mark on the wall. This is your vertical for the first length, allowing the paper to turn 1 inch on to the window wall.

Measure the height from skirting to picture rail (or ceiling if there is no rail), add 2 inches and measure off your first length and cut it. Then you have a choice of ways of matching, if you have to. Either lay the first length on the table, pattern up, and place the paper on the roll alongside it and mark where this length must be cut. Or hang your first piece, then offer the roll up to the wall and mark. The latter is the method I always adopt, but it is purely a matter of choice.

Place your length of paper on the table so that the top of the piece hangs over the edge to your right, then pull the paper to the front edge of the table. Paste the paper—herring bone fashion to within $\frac{1}{2}$ inch of the edges. Then finish pasting the front edge. Now push the paper to the rear of the table and finish pasting the rear edge. This way you will avoid getting paste on the table.

Should you get any paste on the table, lift the paper and wipe it up before pulling the remainder of the paper on to the table. Fold over the surplus paper already pasted and allow it to touch, paste on paste. Complete pasting the length.

Now, if the paper is going straight on to the wall, you can lift the paper by the top and move to the wall. If the paper is to be left to soak, fold in the right hand side to meet the left hand fold so that no paste is visible.

Now to hang the first length. Move to the wall and offer the right hand edge to your chalk mark, holding the left hand edge away from the wall. When you are sure the paper is following the line, smooth upwards to press the rest of the top of the paper to the wall. With the paper in place, undo the fold, and use your hand, or the hanging brush, to sweep down the centre of the length. Then brush outwards, herring bone fashion to get the paper down. Press the paper into the corner, then ease the spare inch down on the window wall.

If the corner was out of true, you will find you have, perhaps $\frac{1}{4}$ inch at the top and 1 inch at the bottom. Don't worry. The first length on the window wall can overlap this turn completely.

Smooth over the length, feeling for bubbles, then press the top and bottom overlap into the angle of skirting and picture rail (or ceiling). Pull the paper away, and carefully trim with scissors, being careful not to tear the damp paper. If there is a slight gap at the skirting board, leave on an extra $\frac{1}{8}$ inch of paper to turn on to the paintwork and thus hide the gap.

Now paste and hang the second piece and match it to the first, this time holding the right hand edge well clear of the wall. Continue until the next corner is reached.

Where a pattern repeat does not go economically into a wall height, try alternating rolls of paper. In this way you may save quite a bit of waste.

When the next corner is reached, don't turn more than a couple of inches unless you are sure the corner is true, or unless you are experienced. Far better cut the paper to turn by an inch, then apply the remaining strip. Trying to turn half a width on a faulty corner means the paper has to be ripped to remove the creases, and this is not an easy job for a beginner.

Work until you reach the corner opposite the one you started on, then return to the window wall and work around the other way. If paper is proving a bit tight, save sections under window sills or above the window until last, where cut pieces can be utilised.

Light switches are a challenge. In the modern home with flush switches, loosen off the holding screws to give a gap of about $\frac{1}{8}$ inch between switch and wall. Feel for the corners of the switch through the paper; make a mark, then cut diagonally each way. Press the paper around the switch, then cut $\frac{3}{8}$ inch inside the creased area. Now press the paper behind the switch with a matchstick and screw up the holding screws. Don't use a metal implement!

If yours are the old switches proud of the wall, mark the area through the paper, cut out star-shaped from the centre, press the paper around the switch, then trim off the surplus.

Apart from standard wallpapers, you will come across all kinds of refinements such as clean stripping papers, washable papers, vinyl wallcoverings, and flock finishes. It is difficult to give precise instructions for all these

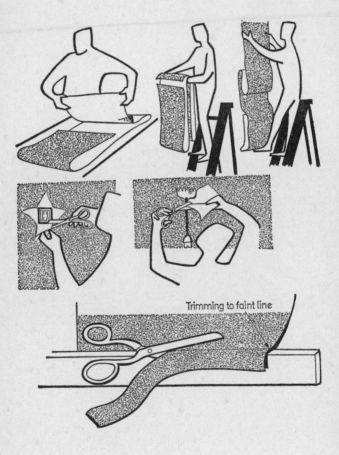

Trimming to faint line

materials, so when considering, or purchasing, be sure to get instructions as to hanging, trimming and which paste to use. Also, Continental wallpapers do not conform to our roll sizes in all cases. If you look in the front of Continental pattern books, you will find details of widths, lengths and special instructions.

A few final tips. As you trim, gather up the cut pieces while the adhesive is still soft. Far easier than scraping dried paper from the floor. Also wipe any paste from paintwork while the paste is wet. Keep a few pieces of paper for repair work, and for reference when choosing carpet or curtains. Should you have to tear paper to make it fit, note that when you tear you will get one white edge and one undercut edge depending how you tear. Make sure the undercut edge goes on top.

Tiling

The introduction of the thin ceramic tile especially for the do-it-yourself market revolutionised wall tiling. The thicker tiles had to be set into cement grouting, but today ceramic tiles can be stuck to any clean, dry surface with adhesive. You can stick to glass, hardboard or plaster with equally good results.

The standard tile is $4\frac{1}{4}$ inches by $4\frac{1}{4}$ inches by $\frac{5}{32}$ inch thick, and it incorporates spacing lugs on each edge so that the correct spacing between tiles is automatically set. After tiling, the gap between tiles is sealed with a special grouting.

For a first attempt, stick to tiling a small area, such as the splash back for a wash basin. For small areas, three tiles plus their spacing lugs equals 13 inches, but for larger areas, refer to the chart.

HOW MANY TILES DO YOU NEED?

Tiles are $4\frac{1}{4}$ inches $\times$ $4\frac{1}{4}$ inches, and each tile is fitted with the special self-spacing lugs on all four sides.

If you are concerned only with a small area, then three tiles plus their spacing lugs = 13 inches

For larger areas, measure the height and width of the area to be tiled, and check your measurements with the following table: —

Tiles	Measurement ft. in.		Tiles	Measurement ft. in.	
1		$4\frac{1}{4}$	13	4	8
2		$8\frac{9}{16}$	14	5	$0\frac{5}{16}$
3	1	$0\frac{7}{8}$	15	5	$5\frac{5}{8}$
4	1	$5\frac{3}{16}$	16	5	$8\frac{15}{16}$
5	1	$9\frac{1}{2}$	17	6	$1\frac{1}{4}$
6	2	$1\frac{13}{16}$	18	6	$5\frac{9}{16}$
7	2	$6\frac{1}{8}$	19	6	$9\frac{7}{8}$
8	2	$10\frac{7}{16}$	20	7	$2\frac{3}{16}$
9	3	$2\frac{3}{4}$	25	8	$11\frac{3}{4}$
10	3	$7\frac{1}{16}$	30	10	$9\frac{5}{16}$
11	3	$11\frac{3}{8}$	36	12	$11\frac{3}{16}$
12	4	$3\frac{11}{16}$			

For edges and corners, use special tiles. (It is not necessary for these fitting-tiles to be self-spacing.)

Apart from many attractive plain colours, you can get tiles in a variety of textures and finishes. And there are special feature tiles, either as singles or designed as panels. Single tiles, such as fruit, fish or flower designs, can look most effective if put in almost at random in a large area of plain tiling.

Special edge tiles are also available for finishing off a tiled area neatly, and at the time of writing a new tile design is being introduced with lugs on only two sides, so one tile can be used for both edges and in-fill.

Adhesive may be applied in one of three ways. It can be put on the wall with a special notched trowel; it can be applied to the back of the tiles in three strips, or it can be put on the tiles as five blobs—one at each corner and one in the centre. I think the blob method is perfectly adequate on good wall surfaces, and it is economical on adhesive. Where rather irregular walls are encountered, you can get a special thick bed adhesive which will fill in the irregularities and help present a smooth tiled surface, but it does need some practice, as the glaze on a tiled surface shows up any variation in surface level.

Before tiling, ensure that you have a level surface to work from. The top of a washbasin will probably be adequate for a base, but when working on a wall from the ground to perhaps half-way up, it is wise to form a start line which is really true. Measure up from the floor one tile width (plus spacers) and make a pencil mark. Lay a dead true piece of batten on the wall so the pencil mark touches the top edge, and place a builder's level on the batten. Get the batten truly horizontal and make another pencil mark.

Now nail the batten temporarily to the wall using masonry nails. Don't hammer them right home. This batten now forms the base for your tiling. Position each tile by one edge then press in place. Don't slide the tile or push too hard or you will get adhesive up between the cracks. Your batten will support the weight of tiling until the adhesive has set.

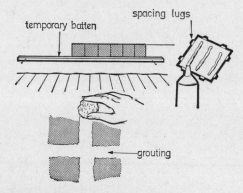

temporary batten

spacing lugs

grouting

Leave the tiling overnight, then take off the batten and fill in the lower row. You may find some tiles won't fit due to an irregular floor. In this case the tiles must be trimmed.

To cut tiles, use a tile cutter and straight-edge. The cutter should just whisper across the glazed surface of the tile. Then place the tile over the edge of the table and lightly press. The tile will snap along the cut. Small areas can be nibbled off with a pair of pincers, but do a little practising first on an old tile.

With the tiling complete, mix up grouting cement and press it into the cracks with a piece of sponge. Don't worry if it goes on the tile faces. When dry, polish over with a pad of screwed-up newspaper. This will remove all the surplus grouting and leave a really lovely shine.

Timber Panelling

In recent years, there has been a general return to a natural timber look in our homes—probably in an attempt to get away from the many synthetic finishes available today. So timber panelling has become very popular, and providing a room is not too small it can add a real touch of luxury and warmth. It is not a cheap wallcovering, but bearing in mind it only needs doing once and that no maintenance is thereafter required, it is a good investment.

I mentioned small rooms because timber panelling does tend to close a room in a little, and in a small room it can become overbearing and make the room look even smaller.

There are a number of ways you can approach panelling. You can buy quite ordinary whitewood floorboarding with tongues and grooves and mount this on a simple timber framing. This, when coated with varnish or polyurethane seal, can look very effective in kitchen or bathroom, and the more knots the better, providing they are not likely to drop out.

Alternatively you can buy plywood strips which have a high quality veneer surface. These are available in a number

of woods, and when pinned to a framing, they look most
effective. Yet another alternative, and perhaps the most
common today, is to buy full panels of plywood, perhaps
8 feet by 4 feet, which are veneered with an attractive wood
then grooved and painted to give a plank effect. Planks may
be regularly sized or varied, but once on the wall it is hard
to distinguish the result from individual planking.

Most panelling is treated already with a seal or varnish,
so there is no finishing to do, and each type has its own instructions supplied with regard to securing to the wall.

The most common fixing method is to secure a simple
framework of battens to the wall with masonry nails, using

batten spacings recommended by the particular manufacturer. Then the panelling is pinned or glued to the battens.
Some panels can be nailed through the tongues at the edges
so that nails are hidden when the next sheet is applied.

Yet another approach is to use special anchor plates.
These are stuck to the wall with adhesive so that short,
sharp spikes are left sticking from the wall. The timber
panel is then tapped on to the spikes, using a rubber
hammer, where the panel is held firmly in place. If a wall is
really flat, it is possible to stick the panels direct to the wall.

Before panelling, consider very carefully whether you
want wall lights, or whether power sockets must be re-sited.
Far better sort out wiring before panels are put on.

Apart from natural timber panels, you can now buy a

wide variety of imitation panellings where a photographically reproduced woodgrain is applied to melamine, hardboard or even cheap grade timber or plywood. If you choose this type, try to ensure that the photo reproduction does not repeat at regular intervals, panel by panel, or you finish up with an effect rather resembling wallpaper.

Speaking of wallpaper, there are papers and vinyls with very realistic woodgrain effects and imitation panellings. Ideal if you want simulated panelling without the expense of the real thing—but don't expect people to be deceived. Nothing looks like real, well-finished timber panelling.

8 Floors

As far as everyday living is concerned, floors take probably
more punishment than any other part of the house structure, and the fact that they are in very close proximity
to the ground adds to the hazards. There are two main
types of floor construction, and each has its own problems,
so we will deal with them separately.

Solid Floors

As the name implies, the solid floor is built up on a solid
base of concrete, and you will see from the illustration that
it incorporates a sandwich layer of damp proof course
material between the coarse concrete and the finer finishing
layer. At least, it should include a damp proof barrier but
if you buy a really old property there may be none, or it
may have broken down. The damp proof barrier should be
linked with the damp proof course in the walls so that
there is no chance of damp creeping through at any point.

Should there be no damp proof layer, moisture may
percolate up until it reaches the top layer of the floor. It will
then attack floorcoverings such as lino or carpet, or form
pools under materials such as vinyl sheeting. Thus, cracking
lino, or mildew and musty smells from carpets will indicate
trouble. But if you have vinyl floorcoverings, it will pay you
to lift a corner occasionally to see that all is well below.

There can be some confusion in diagnosing rising damp,
for during cold weather you can get condensation forming
on the surface of concrete floors. To decide which trouble
you have, get a square of glass about 6 inches square and
bed this firmly on a little wall of putty so that air is trapped

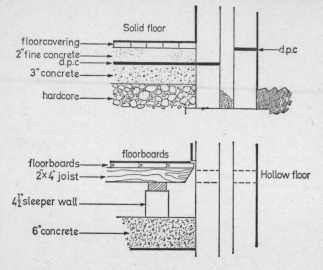

in a sealed space under the glass. Get the glass within about ½ inch of the floor. Examine the glass the following day, and if there is condensation on the underside of the glass, this will be moisture which has come up through the floor. If there is condensation on the top of the glass, this will be condensed moisture from the room air.

Condensation can be quite a problem in homes where there is a lot of moisture-laden air about, and I have heard of cases where it has even formed on carpets despite the carpet's insulating effects. If yours is condensation trouble, read how to combat it in chapter 7.

If you have rising damp, this can be combated by brushing the concrete free of all loose and flaking material, then treating it with a damp resisting material designed to deal with this kind of trouble. The older remedy was to lay a damp proof membrane, then raise the level of the floor by adding an extra 2 inches of fine concrete. But this presents problems with removing skirting boards and re-hanging doors. The liquid treatment will cure all but the most severe cases of rising damp.

In a few cases where a house is situated in a hollow, and there is a tendency for water to drain towards the house, you may have to contend with what is termed hydrostatic pressure, where water is literally forced up through the floor under quite considerable pressure. Where such a problem is encountered, you really need professional help. Call in your borough surveyor to advise.

In some homes, you get just a very slight evaporation of moisture from a concrete floor—maybe just enough to give a musty smell to floorcovering and perhaps encourage mould growth on nearby paintwork. Such a situation can be encountered in rooms above garages, where the law has demanded a concrete roof to the garage—and thus you have a concrete floor to a cold bedroom. When a car is put away wet, water will evaporate off and possibly find its way through the ceiling. And, as the floor will tend to be cold as there is no heating below, you could get condensation as well. In such a case, and with any slightly damp floor, cover the floor with a bitumen/latex compound—two or three coats if possible. Then lay over this a building paper which has a reflective foil surface, with the foil uppermost.

If you put underlay and carpet, or cork underlay and lino or vinyl over such a base, you should get no more trouble.

Another fault encountered with solid floors is crumbling of the surface or uneven areas due to faulty laying. Here again, modern methods simplify treatment, for you can buy a screeding compound which can be spread over the floor to give a new surface. The floor should be clean and dry, and the compound trowelled over to the thickness recommended by the particular manufacturer. Usually layers are meant to be thin, but if you want to build up a surface you can add special fillers to the mix to bulk it up.

Most materials are what is called self-levelling, which is of tremendous advantage to the amateur as it means that trowel marks and minor irregularities disappear as the layer finds its own level.

Where old quarry tiles, bricks, or other building materials are encountered as floorcoverings—and this applies in many older properties in country districts—you can use a screeding compound to provide a new level over which you can lay any floorcovering. You don't need to lift the old materials apart from digging out loose and flaking pieces.

Where a floor is not too regular, but where you don't wish to lay a screeding compound, you can cover the floor with sheet hardboard preferably bonded in place to save any noise between the two layers. Providing the floor is dry, you can use a standard grade board. If you have any doubts, lay a coating of bitumen/latex, then follow with another coat to act as an adhesive for the board. If you prefer not to fix the board, just lay a building paper and put the hardboard on top of this. It is wise to give generous overlaps in the paper.

Yet another very effective treatment for a fairly regular but unattractive concrete floor is to lay parquet blocks in bitumen adhesive straight on to the floor. The adhesive has enough body to cushion the blocks from any minor irregularities, but you would be wise to go over the floor first to chip down any projections. You can use a steel chisel and club hammer for this job. You can also lay tongued and grooved boards in the same way.

Where you don't wish to bond parquet to the floor, you can buy special tongued and grooved panels which can be laid loose on the floor, yet present a very firm, durable surface. Such blocks can be lifted if you move, but it is not the easiest of jobs to separate blocks that have been tapped together.

Where a concrete floor is in good shape, smooth and dry, then any floorcovering can be added. If you should prefer just to paint it, you can buy very tough rubber-based paints which will give extremely good wear.

Hollow Floors

Very many homes have a suspended timber floor as illustrated at the beginning of this chapter, with a cavity below
the floor varying in depth from a matter of inches to four
or five feet. Basically, there will be an area of concrete upon
which are built open or honeycomb walls called sleeper
walls. On these walls are laid the floor joists so that they are
supported at regular intervals. Each wall will incorporate a
damp proof course so that rising damp cannot reach the
timber, and you will also see that air bricks in the outer walls
ensure that the underfloor space is well ventilated. Though
mentioned elsewhere, it is worth stressing here that these
airbricks should not be obstructed—even during winter
months. All the time ventilation is good, no harm should
come to the timber, but if you cut off the flow of air, conditions are then ideal for rot spores to get a grip.

If your home has hollow ground floors, your main con-
cern will be with the floorboards fixed to the joists. If you
have trouble with actual joists, be it rot or joists not bedding correctly on the supporting walls, call in expert help.

Boards encountered are of two main types; butted, and
tongued and grooved. Butted boards are usually encountered in older properties, and here the boards are merely
pressed close together, then secured. With tongued and
grooved boards the floorboards actually interlock, eliminat-
ing gaps through which draughts can pass. Let us look at
some of the faults you may encounter.

Butted boards may have contracted with age or through
the installation of central heating, leaving quite considerable gaps between, through which draughts can pass. Of
course the boards could be lifted and re-nailed, but this
would be a marathon job. Far better either to fill the gaps
or lay a new floorcovering over the top. Gaps may be filled
by chamfering batten to a wedge shape until it can be tapped
into cracks. Apply glue to the batten, tap home, allow to
dry, then level off with a plane or shaping tool. Smaller

cracks can be filled by the time-honoured method of making up a papier mâché. Shred up old newspaper and soak in water. Drain off the water and mash the paper to a pulp. Squeeze off the water, then add a mixture of glue size and water to form a putty-like mix. This can be pressed into cracks with an old knife and allowed to set, when it can be rubbed down with glasspaper. Such a mix can be coloured by adding water-based stain to the mixture, but bear in mind that such stains tend to dry a little darker than you expect. A little experimenting is well worth while.

If you prefer to cover over, standard hardboard will do fine. This can be stuck down with a suitable flooring adhesive, but if you plan to do this, check whether you may need access to wiring, gas or water pipes below the boards. Sometimes it is an idea to fit panels at suitable spots using fine screws instead of adhesive. Pinning is never very successful with hardboard, as natural flexing of the floor tends to pull loose the pins.

Where a board has hollowed with wear, it may either need replacing, or you may be able to lift the board and turn it over. Either way, you will have to lift up the old floorboard, and this is no easy task until you get some experience.

Butted boards are easiest. Insert an old chisel blade between boards near a joist (you can spot joist positions by the nails) and lever up to lift the nails. If the floorboard nails are rusted well in and protest, it may be simpler to knock the nails down into the joists using a hammer and punch. While this process is suitable for ground floors, I do not recommend it with floors higher up a house as the vibration could bring down ceiling plaster from a room below!

In some cases you may have to cut a board across before you can lift. Use a tenon saw or sheet saw close by the side of a joist—or if you are experienced, you can use a power saw. Do work cautiously if you are not sure where cables run or gas and water pipes pass! The idea of cutting close

Batten nailed to floor joist to support
board when replaced

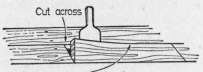

Cut across

Cut through tongue then lever up

to a joist is so that when you come to replace the cut board
or insert a new piece, you can nail a piece of batten to the
joist to form a ledge upon which the replaced floor board can
rest.

If you have to lift a tongued and grooved board, the job
is a little more complex. You must cut along the board on
one side to cut through the tongue joining them. A sheet
saw is ideal for the job, and again caution is advised to
avoid cutting through something you shouldn't.

With the tongue cut through, lever out from the side
very carefully. You may have to lift the nails, or you may
have to sink them into the joists as previously mentioned.
If you are careful you may not damage the joint on the
other side of the board, but where a fit is tight, you may
wreck the tongue. You will note when you get a board up
that the tongue is not centrally sited. It is in fact off-centre,
and you must bear this in mind when putting down a new
board.

You will also see that a new tongued and grooved board
is not going to go in without trimming. You may be able to
get the new tongue home, then cut off the underside of the
groove—or you may be able to insert the groove, then note
how much tongue you must cut away. The first method

offers the best result. Once in place, a new piece of board
can be nailed in, but again, if working on any but the ground
floor, I would advise screwing to prevent damage to the ceiling below. It is also a very good idea to screw back boards
that have been lifted when installing cable or pipe—such as
for central heating. Then if you ever need to get at the spot
for servicing or repair, the board can be easily lifted.

Even in tongued and grooved boards, drying out of timber can cause considerable gaps between them. This is particularly noticeable when central heating is installed and
the moisture content of timber is considerably reduced.
Gaps may be filled with papier mâché as previously mentioned, or you may prefer to cover with board.

Where a floor is in very poor shape, it may have to be
lifted and new flooring laid. You may feel this is too big a
job to tackle, but if you do decide to do it yourself it is
worth considering using a sheet flooring in place of floorboard. The job can be done faster, and you have not the
problem of pressing individual boards tight together. There
are special flooring grades of chipboard which are excellent
for floor covering—and in fact this material is used in many
modern homes.

If you choose such a sheet material, do remember the
problem of likely inspections under the floors, and have
screwed panels at vital spots.

A less serious but just as annoying problem is that of
squeaking floorboards. In most serious cases it may be the
actual floor joist loose in a wall socket so that the whole
floor moves. In this case the joist will have to be wedged up
tight, and this you may feel is a job for the expert. But in
most cases it is only the actual floorboard which is loose in
relation to the joist so that two boards rub together. You
can usually cure the trouble by putting in screws at noisy
spots so that the board is pulled tight to the joist.

If there is no joist near enough, you can often stop noise
by screwing a suitable screw with lots of thread and little
shank down between the boards. The thread on the screw

will bite into both boards, preventing movement. Where even this is not possible, lubrication can help. Puff some talc or french chalk into the gap, or give a squirt from one of the new wood lubricants supplied in aerosol form. These are silicone-based, and are now widely used for cutting friction between timber surfaces.

Don't use nails for squeaks, as they tend to pull under strain—unless you use what are called ring nails, which are very difficult indeed to lift at some later date. And when you do use screws, remember to countersink them well into the timber so the heads do not spoil any floor-covering material.

Where a floor is in good shape, but a little uneven, you can give it a new lease of life by hiring a professional sanding machine for a day or two. These machines take a belt of tough abrasive material, and there is a built-in suction unit which collects the dust rather like a vacuum cleaner. The abrasives come in a number of grades from coarse to fine, and when you hire the machine, the hire company will supply suitable abrasives and tell you which order to use them in. Such a machine is not difficult to use, and it will save days of manual work.

The sander can also be used on dirty or neglected parquet or strip hardwood flooring, bringing it up like new—but be sure to get advice on the right abrasives for the job. You don't want to get deep scratches in a nice hardwood parquet.

A word should be added here to the effect that wherever you plan to re-surface, by hand or power, have a thorough search over the floor for nails, pins, tacks or staples standing proud. These would quickly ruin abrasives and perhaps backing pads, and you can get some very nasty cuts if you catch your hand.

Laying Floorcoverings

Assuming that your floor is in good condition, dry and smooth, you can lay floorcovering of your choice. But with all of them, the smoother the foundation, the better the appearance and wear. For this reason, if a floor is uneven or if boards have worn, covering the surface with hardboard will help considerably.

If you have no experience of laying floorcovering, it is wise to consider the use of tiles. You can get both hard materials such as linoleum and vinyl, and soft materials such as carpet in tile-form, and because you can work in small squares it is far easier to fit in awkward and confined places.

When you decide to use tiles, first get a leaflet from likely firms on which there is a squared chart. This can be

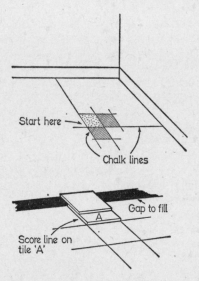

Start here

Chalk lines

Gap to fill

A

Score line on
tile 'A'

used for marking out the area of the room, then calculating how many tiles are required. You can also colour in any pattern you have in mind, again to help you work out how many of each colour are needed.

Bisect the floor each way so that you find a centre point of the room. You can do this with a length of chalked string, and if this is positioned then snapped, a line will be left on the floor. Work from the centre out, and if adhesive is used, do a small area at a time—not too thick. Lower tiles on to the adhesive—don't slide the tiles across it or you will force adhesive up between the tiles. Should you do this by mistake, clean it off before it sets.

Eventually you will have to cut tiles to fit, and this can be done as shown in the illustration. Lay a full tile over the last full laid tile. Put another tile on top and slide it to the wall. Mark with a pencil the edge of the top tile on the under tile and cut to the line. The cut piece will fit the gap.

Where awkward shapes have to be cut, the ideal aid is a tool called a template former. This has a row of very fine plated needles held under tension between two plates, and when the needles are pressed on to an irregular shape, such as a moulding, the needles take up the exact shape, and this can be drawn off on to a tile. An alternative is to make a simple template from brown paper, trimming until it fits, then drawing the shape.

Sheet material is far more difficult to handle, especially in confined spaces. Leave vinyls and linoleums in the warm before use and they will be easier to handle, and be sure to measure twice and cut once! A mistake here can result in awkward patching. If strips must be added, try to position them away from traffic, doorways or furniture which has to be moved about.

Sheet materials give best results if stuck down with an adhesive recommended by the makers of the floorcovering, and if they are stuck down, there is no need to allow for expansion or contraction of the sheeting. Again avoid getting adhesive on the surface of the material. Where trimming must be done, use a lino knife. This has a special curved blade which will cut through sheet materials easily and safely. Keep your hands behind the cutting blade all the same to avoid accidents.

Where a sheet material is to be laid loose, you must give the material time to adjust itself before final trimming.

Lino expands and should be left a couple of weeks to tread down. Vinyl contracts, so you need a bit of spare to fill any gap that may form over a couple of weeks.

Even if the covering is to be laid loose, the edges must be secured. Carpet tape will do the job simply and efficiently, or if you want a more positive bond, use double-sided carpet tape which will bond the material to the floor. If you can't get double-sided tape, you can fold pieces back on itself to form a sort of loop with the adhesive on the outside.

Sheet carpet is far more tricky to lay, especially if it is to be fitted over the complete floor. It really should be stretched taut, and to do this a special carpet stretching tool is required. You may be able to hire one from a good hire shop, but failing this, it will pay you to get a professional in to fix it for you. Special carpet gripping rods are available which can be secured to timber or concrete, then when the carpet is stretched, it is tucked down behind the gripper, where it is held firmly in place by specially shaped teeth.

Professional joins are sewn up, but adhesive binding tape will give a good join, and it can be used for finishing cut edges too. Tacks may have to be used in certain places, in which case use ones with large heads, and space them evenly so that there is no strain on any one section.

You will find a lino knife useful for cutting carpet, for the curved blade will cut without damaging underfelt below.

Carpet squares are best anchored too, and if you don't want to use tacks, strips of Velcro tape can be used. This is in two parts, a sort of looped tape and a hooked tape. One part of the tape is fixed to the underside of the carpet, and the other to the floor by adhesive. When the two tapes are pressed together they grip firmly—yet can be ripped apart when necessary. This tape is also ideal for positioning runners and rugs on polished floors such as parquet. It will stop them moving.

At doorways, all floorcoverings are best protected to prevent the edge getting kicked up. You can buy special

lino or carpet edging strips for such locations, and there are
various types to meet any need. The strip is merely cut to
doorway width, located over the edge of the floorcovering,
then screwed down.

9 Ceilings

In older property, ceilings will probably be of lath and plaster construction. This is shown in the illustration, and you will find that laths are nailed to the ceiling joists, with a gap left between each, then plaster containing hair to bind it is forced up from below so that the plaster is squeezed up between the laths. It turns over slightly, forming a key which holds the plaster in place. When set, a skim coat of plaster adds a smooth finish.

Such a ceiling will give years of service, but houses which had to survive the last war may well have had a severe shaking, breaking the plaster key. The same may apply where heavy hammering or severe jolts have been applied to the

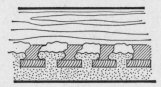

floor above. Once this key is damaged, the plaster will sag away, and may even break off in pieces.

Where a ceiling is sagging—and you can soon tell by getting up close and pressing the plaster up—you can often effect a repair by drilling holes in the plaster and driving rust-proof screws up through the laths or into the joists. This will pull the plaster up. Or you may be able to wedge the area up from underneath with a piece of board and length of timber, then pour plaster in liquid form down on the laths from above to form a new key. This is assuming you can get at the ceiling.

Where the plaster has broken up, there is nothing for it but to pull away loose pieces and re-plaster the area, forming a key as described. This is not an easy job, and you may prefer to call in professional help.

It is possible to disguise a repaired ceiling by a number of means. You can paper the ceiling with a fairly heavy *Anaglypta* paper with a textured surface which will hide irregularities. Or you can stipple the ceiling with a special plastic paint (not to be confused with emulsion paint). This is spread on like lemon curd, then pulled up with a wooden float or patterned with a special comb—or even with screwed up rag—to give a textured finish. Such a coating can look very effective, but it is wise to consider that such a layer is practically impossible to remove at a later date.

If you have to remove such a coating, a steam stripper is the best method. Ordinary scraping is useless.

As a last resort with a poor ceiling that is holding up well, you can cover it with expanded polystyrene tiles— either plain or textured. If possible use the non-flam grades which won't support a flame even if they do disappear.

Where a lath and plaster ceiling is in really poor shape, the only cure is to pull down all the old plaster, rip off all the laths, then cover the ceiling with plasterboard. This is a big job; it is extremely messy, and it is very tiring on the arms! You may prefer to get in some help here.

In newer property, ceilings are constructed of sheet plasterboard applied direct to the joists and nailed in place with special large headed nails which sink into the surface. A special paper face forms a decorative surface for the ceiling, but today it is very common for plasterboard ceilings to be covered with the plastic paint already mentioned and stippled to hide joints and nail depressions.

Such ceilings usually give little trouble, and the most common fault is cracking along joints due to house move-

ment or too much weight being applied above. This is often
noted below a loft when the loft is loaded with lots of heavy
material. Mere filling with a cellulose filler is not much
help, as further flexing will loosen the filler. Far better to
cover the ceiling with a lining paper, then cover with an
Anaglypta textured paper. It is then unlikely that the cracking will re-appear. Of course another safe way of hiding
cracks is to use some form of ceiling tile over the plaster.
Again, expanded polystyrene will do fine, but there are
other types of tile such as fibre board, textured plaster or
strawboard. The main disadvantage of the later types is
the extra weight imposed on the ceiling and the difficulty
of securing them.

One common trouble on ceilings is staining. This may be
caused in bedrooms by a leaking roof, damaged water
storage tanks. Dirt, and perhaps rust deposits, soak through
the plaster leaving unpleasant stains on the ceiling which
seem to re-appear every time they are covered over. Leaking pipes or radiators may cause similar stains on down-
stairs ceilings.

Of course the first job is to clear up the trouble and let
the plaster dry out. Then the stained area should be painted
with aluminium paint of the scale variety which will seal
off the discoloured area. Once this paint is dry, the plaster
may be painted or papered, and the stain will not re-appear.

Any house tends to move very slightly on its foundations according to time of year as the ground dries out or
becomes more waterlogged. A house built on clay can move
quite alarmingly when weather conditions go to extremes
between flooding and prolonged drought. When movement takes place, it must appear somewhere, and one weak
spot is the joint between walls and ceiling.Cracking can
appear here time after time, despite careful filling and painting.

To hide such cracks, and to improve greatly the general
appearance of a room, you can put up a cove cornice which
will bridge the corner.

There are three main types from which to choose; expanded polystyrene, *Anaglypta,* and gypsum coving.

The expanded polystyrene is the easiest to fix, but it has the disadvantage that it is supplied in short lengths, usually 3 feet, and it is very hard to hide the joints. In fact it is best just to ignore them rather than try to smooth down or fill in. Lengths are fixed with special adhesive, and you can buy internal and external corners to match, making corner turning very easy.

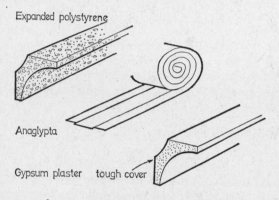

Expanded polystyrene

Anaglypta

Gypsum plaster   tough cover

The second type, *Anaglypta* cove cornice, is supplied by the roll, rather resembling a roll of moulded cardboard. It can be cut to length as required, with no joins, and a special template is supplied for cutting the internal and external angles. Fixing is by means of a special adhesive called *Dextrine,* rather resembling lemon curd, and as the adhesive takes a while to set, the coving must be held in place by small panel pins. The pins can be taken out next day. One disadvantage with this coving is that it has no raised edge, and thus no ledge up to which paper from wall and ceiling can be neatly finished. One big advantage is the price: very reasonable.

By far the most attractive coving is the gypsum one. Made of a core of gypsum covered in stiff material like grey cardboard, it is available in lengths long enough to cover most rooms with no joins. A special template is supplied for marking the mitres for corners, and it is as well to get some practice in before cutting full lengths.

The cove is fairly heavy, so you will need help in getting it in place, but despite this there is a special adhesive which gives an immediate bond, so the cove can be offered up to the wall and ceiling and there it will stay with no nails or pins to hold it. This coving has a good step, so paper looks neat when taken to it.

With all coving, you need to bond to bare wall and ceiling plaster—not to old paper, so clean off old paper back far enough to achieve this. The best time to put up the coving is after stripping walls of paper and before re-papering.

Once up, the coving can be painted to match or contrast with proposed decoration. If you prefer it, coving by the pack in short lengths is now available.

Ceiling tiles are applied to a ceiling rather like you would tile a floor; by bisecting the walls and snapping a chalk line to give you a centre point. Work from the centre out if the room is fairly well balanced, but where tiles will have to be cut it sometimes is as well to put full tiles where they are most noticed, and do the cutting where you are least likely to look.

Your ceiling must be perfectly clean and dry, and any distemper or other chalky paint must be scrubbed off or the adhesive will lose its grip. Apply adhesive over the whole tile area—not in blobs. An over-all cover gives best security against fire damage, and is now the only way recommended by the Fire Protection Association. If you have to cut tiles, use a sharp razor blade and straight-edge, or you can use a hot wire cutter when shaping is necessary.

Where you wish to paint expanded polystyrene tiles, the job is best done prior to putting them up. Far easier, and there is no problem with getting into cracks. It is worth remembering that many non-flam tiles are affected by emulsion paint, which reduces or eliminates their non-flam qualities.

Don't use oil-based paints on expanded polystyrene, it tends to destroy the cell structure, and it adds to fire risk.

If you just wish to paint the ceiling, a lining paper will always improve the general appearance, though many people do not bother where a ceiling is in good shape. Use emulsion paint or acrylic paint applied by roller or pad brush. If you use a roller, keep the speed down or you will spatter the room. Where a textured paper is to be painted, a shaggy lambswool roller will get into the crevices best.

Papering a Ceiling

Applying paper to a ceiling is a little tricky as you have gravity added to your problems! So the first essential is to have a working platform with your head just clear of the ceiling by an inch or two. A stout plank on two heavy boxes, or a pair of steps and a box will do.

If you choose a paper which has no real pattern, you can start from one wall and move over to the other in strips. But where there is a definite pattern it is better to start at the centre of the ceiling and work out either way.

Always work parallel with the window wall, and if there is no pattern to worry about, start at the window and work in strips away from it. This way you will avoid getting shadows should the paper overlap even slightly.

Assuming you are starting from a wall, measure in from the wall the width of the paper less $\frac{1}{8}$ inch and strike a line with your chalked string. The paper will be hung to this line and you will get just a slight turn on to the wall or coving. By measurement, cut a number of paper lengths, place the first on the pasting table with the bulk to your right, and as you paste, pull the paper over to the left and fold concertina-wise until the whole length is pasted.

Such a weight of pasted paper needs support, so slide a spare roll under the paper so that it drapes over the roll.

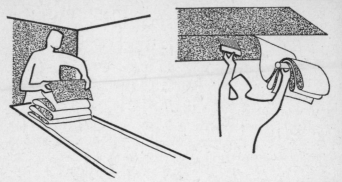

You can thus use the roll to carry the paper to the ceiling. Release the first small fold, offer the paper to the ceiling, then turn and work ahead, brushing the paper in place from the centre as you go, the remaining paper still supported on the roll, and held in front and a little below the line of advance.

With the paper up, brush out herring bone fashion to ensure the paper is smooth and free from blisters, then trim off the surplus at each end.

Now continue, strip by strip, to the far end. The light switch or switches, may prove a little tricky, but by careful measurement you can make a star-shaped cut through which the fitting can pass before you paste the paper. Don't forget to allow for the extra piece for trimming, or you will have your star a few inches out of position. With the fitting through, press the paper around the fitting, pull away and cut just a fraction inside the creases so that just a little paper turns on to the fitting. Wipe off paste before it dries.

It is best to butt ceiling papers to avoid shadows and, as with wallpapers, if you choose a relief pattern *Anaglypta*, don't press the edges of the paper down too much or you will get smooth lines along the joins. Remember the next length will have bumps which will match those standing proud already.

CEILINGS

Measurement in feet round room	No. of pieces	Measurement in feet round room	No. of pieces
20	1	60	5
24	1	62	5
26	1	64	5
28	1	66	5
30	2	68	6
32	2	70	6
34	2	74	7
36	2	76	7
38	2	78	7
40	2	80	8
42	3	82	8
44	3	86	9
46	3	88	9
48	3	90	10
52	4	92	10
54	4	96	11
56	4	98	11
58	4	100	12

10 Up Aloft

Assuming you have a loft which is not used as part of your living accommodation, it is wise to give the loft periodic inspections to see that all is well. From this point of view it pays to wire a light that can be switched on from the hatch, and if the loft is used for storage, a good investment is a loft ladder to make access to the loft simple and safe. Many reasonably priced ladders are available which can be fitted quite easily in a standard loft hatch opening.

When in the loft, remember you must not step between joists! The ceiling plaster will not support your weight—or the weight of other heavy objects. To be safe, lay boards over the area most used, and these should be secured with screws—not nails.

Examine the actual roof. In more modern homes there will be a bitumen fabric lining hiding the actual roof tiles from view. This is ideal as the lining keeps out wind and weather. In some homes you may even have boards over the rafters, giving the same effect. But in many older houses, it is possible to see out through the gaps, and during bad weather, wind and rain will get in. Even worse, fine snow can be blown in, and this will later melt, perhaps forming pools and eventual stains on ceilings.

Such a roof can be protected by pinning a waterproof building paper to the rafters. Drawing pins will do. Overlap the paper, and feed the bottom end of each length into the eaves and, if possible push it right through so that collected moisture is fed out of the roof. Some people worry about damp rot with the rafters blocked off like this, but usually there is ample ventilation to keep trouble away. Alterna-

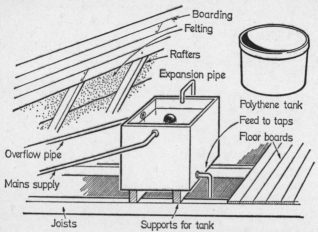

tively you can use sheet plasterboard with a foil surface presented to the outside elements.

Where rafters are visible, examine them for signs of trouble. Rot is not common in a roof, but you may find signs of beetle attack. See 'Woodworm' in chapter 12. Where there is any doubt, call in an expert company to conduct a free survey. They will advise you of the seriousness of any attack, and they will either do the work for you, or you can get the materials and hire a spray to do the work yourself. If a specialist company does the work, you will get a written guarantee of up to 20 years against further attack.

Check also for signs of damp coming in through cracks and gaps. See chapter 2.

If you have central heating, there should be a layer of insulation between the joists. This can be a granular material such as vermiculite; glass fibre matting, mineral wool, expanded polystyrene pellets or sheets, or a special reflective foil. Each manufacturer will advise on recommended thickness of the layer of insulation, but whatever you choose, the money will be recouped in fuel savings.

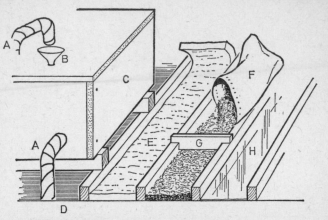

A. All pipes properly lagged
B. Funnel to direct water through lagging
C. Expanded polystyrene tank set (or use glass fibre blanket)
D. Don't insulate under tank
E. Glass fibre blanket
F. —or use vermiculite or mineral wool
G. Simple depth gauge
H. —or use reflective foil

Don't risk using materials like old woollens, fabrics, news-papers or sawdust. True, they have insulating value, but they attract insects and vermin, and they are a potential fire risk.

Insulation of course lowers the loft temperature very considerably during freezing weather, so it is essential to lag all pipes and tanks with a suitable insulation, and see that the cold water storage tank has a cover, plus a layer of insulation on top of the cover.

Check the interior of the cold water tank, and if there are signs of corrosion, tie up the ball valve with string passed around a length of wood rested over the tank, and drain off the water. You will have to mop out the last inch or so, as pipes should be set above the bottom of the tank so that dirt is not carried out. If the tank is sound, it can be coated with a tasteless, odourless bituminous paint to protect it. Give at least two coats. If there are signs of mild corrosion, wire-brush the patches until all loose material is off; make sure the surface is quite dry, then apply a coat of cold galvanizing paint. You could follow this with bitumen once the paint is hard.

If corrosion is bad, replace the the tank before it bursts and causes serious damage. Most tanks are installed before the roof goes on, and it is rare that a metal tank will go out through a hatch or that a new metal one can be lifted in. Fortunately, today there are excellent plastic tanks, either round or square, and these can be compressed to push through a hatch, then plumbed in as for a metal tank.

There are big advantages in plastics as they will not rust, corrode or support vegetable life. But do not heave your way into the loft by means of a pipe connected to a plastic tank. You could end up with a flood!

Finally, if you want to keep the chill off the loft during severe weather, use appliances made for the job. Never use electric reflector fires, paraffin heaters or other devices which could cause a fire. Black heat tubular heaters will keep the chill off a sealed loft, but don't drape anything over them at any time. Pipe runs can be protected by special heating cables or tapes which are only switched on when frost is imminent, and you can also get a special tank immersion heater which will just keep the chill off a tank for very reasonable cost. Any electrical appliances used in areas not immediately visible should be fitted with pilot lights which can be seen to be lit when an appliance is on. It is very easy to forget a heater—until you get the bill for electricity!

Remember that many modern lofts are not designed to take much, if any, weight. The timber sections used are too small. In this case, don't over-do the weight, and spread it as much as possible. If you do want to make more use of the loft, then it may pay to add further timber joists alongside those already there. In this way the floor can be very substantially strengthened. Your borough surveyor could advise on suitable timber sections if you are not too sure.

11 Your Services

Water

The average domestic water system is a very faithful servant. It functions year after year with next to no attention—and because of this few people take the trouble to figure out how it all works until something goes wrong.

Your responsibility for the system starts your side of the water authority's stop cock, and this cock will be situated in a hole in the pavement or road. It will be fitted with a special head which can only be operated by a water authority key. The pipe should then approach your house at least 2 feet 6 inches below ground level to protect it from frost, and it should rise very gradually towards the house so that air is not trapped in the pipe.

The pipe next appears on an inside wall, usually in the kitchen, and at its lowest point you will find a stop cock, with which you can cut off the water supply. Test this cock and see that it turns on and off freely enough for even young members of your family to operate it in an emergency. In many homes the cock won't even move, due to sheer neglect over many years. In modern systems you will find above this cock a special drain cock by means of which the rising main—as the pipe from here on is called—can be drained if necessary.

The cold tap in the kitchen will be taken from this pipe so that you get mains water for cooking and drinking, and in some homes, bathroom cold taps and perhaps a water closet may be connected.

In very large areas, like the Greater London area, toilets must be connected to a storage tank and not to the mains water, so that should the water supply fail, water is still available from the storage tank. The storage tanks also act as a buffer so that the mains are not run dry during peak periods.

The mains pipe now connects to a ball valve in the cold water storage tank, usually in the loft, then all other supply pipes—to the hot water system and to toilets—are connected to this tank. The tank, incidentally, is usually required to have a minimum actual capacity of 25 gallons if it supplies cold water outlets only. If the tank is connected to the hot water system, then it should have a capacity of at least 50 gallons. If you have to order a new tank, remember you are interested in the actual capacity—not in the amount the tank would hold if it were filled to the brim.

Your tank is probably of galvanized iron, and such a tank should be regularly inspected for signs of corrosion. It pays also to empty the tank; dry it out, and coat the interior with two or three coats of tasteless, odourless bituminous paint. With such a coating, the life of the tank will be increased very considerably. You can also cut corrosion by fitting what is called a sacrificial anode. This is a bar of

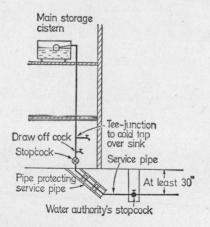

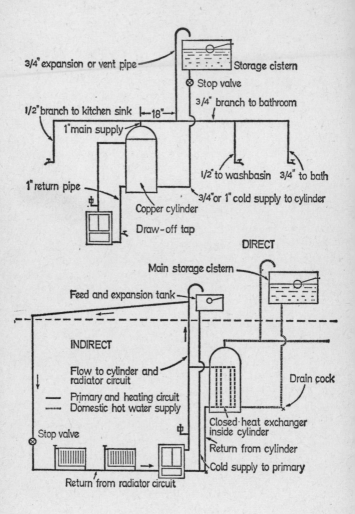

3/4" expansion or vent pipe

Storage cistern

Stop valve

3/4" branch to bathroom

1/2" branch to kitchen sink |←—18"—→|

1" main supply

1/2" to washbasin   3/4" to bath

1" return pipe

3/4" or 1" cold supply to cylinder

Copper cylinder

Draw-off tap

DIRECT

Main storage cistern

Feed and expansion tank

INDIRECT

Flow to cylinder and radiator circuit

Drain cock

——— Primary and heating circuit
········· Domestic hot water supply

Stop valve

Closed heat exchanger inside cylinder

Return from cylinder

Cold supply to primary

Return from radiator circuit

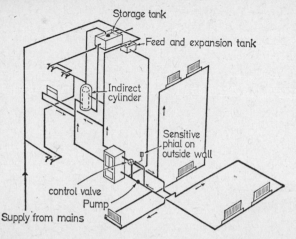

metal connected to the tank and suspended in the water so that the bar is sacrificed and not the tank galvanizing.

If you have to put in a new tank, put in one of the new cylindrical polythene tanks which can't corrode or rust. But they are a little more delicate, so don't heave yourself in the loft by pipes connected to a plastic tank. You could get very wet!

The ball valve is best fitted with a silencer tube which can be screwed into a threaded hole beneath the valve. You can buy a plastic tube at any plumbers' merchants ready-threaded.

There should be a hole in the tube to admit air. This is to prevent back-siphonage should the water supply fail with the valve in the open position.

If the valve dribbles when it is meant to be off, the valve may need renewing. First turn off the water at the mains stop cock, then straighten the split pin holding the arm to the valve; withdraw it and pull out the valve unit. You can buy a replacement at any plumbers' merchant. If the whole unit is ancient and noisy, replacement is not difficult, and it

pays to get a new plastic unit which is quieter in operation
and which allows faster filling. Ask for a *Garston* pattern,
and state whether for mains pressure or tank pressure, for a
similar unit can be used for lavatory cisterns run from the
tank pressure.

The actual ball may give trouble too—especially if you
have the hollow metal type. If it corrodes or splits, water
will enter and the valve will stay open, in which case water

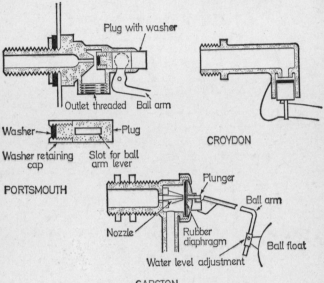

Plug with washer

Outlet threaded   Ball arm

Washer   Plug

Washer retaining   Slot for ball
cap   arm lever

PORTSMOUTH

CROYDON

Plunger

Ball arm

Nozzle   Rubber
         diaphragm   Ball float

Water level adjustment

GARSTON

will flow continually from the overflow pipe. Tie up the ball
arm by placing a length of wood across the tank and string-
ing the ball arm to this. As a temporary repair, empty out
the water, turn the hole uppermost, then slip a polythene
bag over the ball and secure it at the mouth with string.

When getting a replacement ball, buy a plastic one that
can't rust, corrode, or be holed easily.

Taps may need occasional attention, and before touching, study the illustrations of the basic types and note how the screw mechanism works. And with all repair work be very careful to ensure that no pressure applied to the tap is passed to the basin. Also, put the plug in the waste pipe so that small grub screws don't disappear down the hole!

Dripping at the tap handle can often be cured merely by tightening the gland adjusting nut part of a turn. This compresses the packing, sealing off the water. If this fails you may need to re-pack. First turn off the water supply to the tap, then undo the nut and re-pack the space below with wool or string smeared with Vaseline. Replace the gland nut and tighten. Don't go too tight or the tap will be hard to turn on and off.

Rewashering a normal bib tap is not difficult. Turn off the water supply to the tap, then with a suitable spanner, undo the whole of the head gear, applying similar pressure by hand in the opposite direction to that applied by the spanner. The whole head will come away, revealing the jumper with washer attached. If you are dealing with a mains tap, the jumper should be loose and drop away. If the tap is fed by the storage tank, or is a hot tap, the washer may be held in place yet free to turn.

Bath tap washers will probably be $\frac{3}{4}$ inch and other tap washers $\frac{1}{2}$ inch. Cold tap washers are usually leather, and hot ones fibre composition. If in doubt, take the old one with you to the shop.

Many taps have an easy-clean cover, and this is often harder to remove than the rest of the tap as the chromium plating is easily damaged. First remove the grub screw holding the handle in place, and tap off the handle. Then put plenty of cloth or leather padding around the cover before applying the wrench. With the cover removed, proceed as mentioned above.

An exception to most of the rules given above applies when you have Supataps, for these can be re-washered without turning off the water supply. First, a retaining nut is

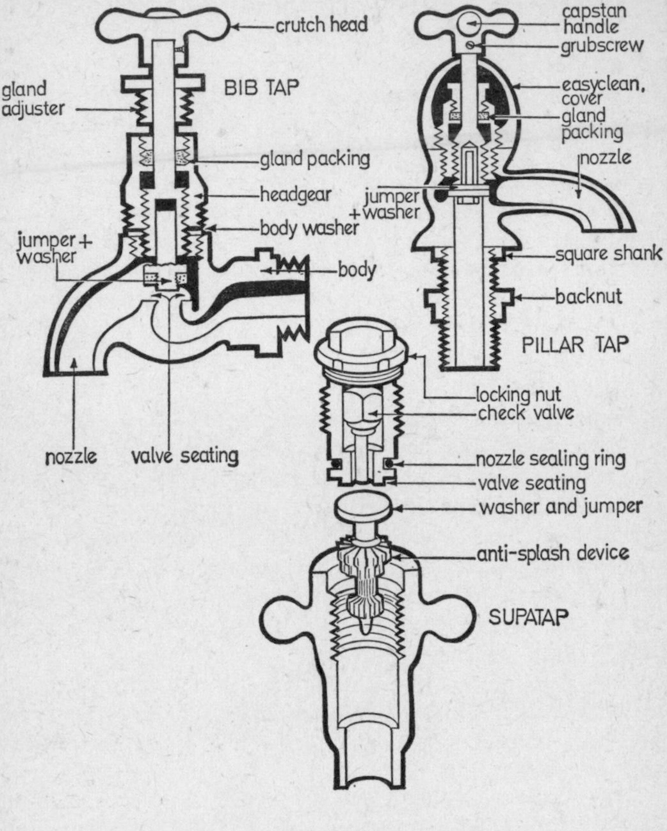

crutch head

BIB TAP

gland
adjuster

gland packing

headgear

body washer

jumper +
washer

jumper +
washer

body

nozzle   valve seating

capstan
handle

grubscrew

easyclean
cover
gland
packing

nozzle

square shank

backnut

PILLAR TAP

locking nut

check valve

nozzle sealing ring

valve seating

washer and jumper

anti-splash device

SUPATAP

unscrewed, then the lower part of the tap turned on and on until it can be removed, complete with washer and anti-splash device. The water may increase alarmingly at first, but it will stop as a special check valve drops into place. With a new washer in place, the operation is reversed.

Sometimes the actual valve seating is damaged so that washers are quickly ruined as they are pressed on to a sharp edge. In such a case you can buy a special nylon washer

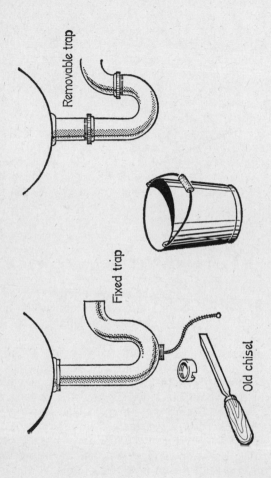

Removable trap

Fixed trap

Old chisel

and valve seating with which to repair the tap. The new seating merely pushes over the old one.

Blocked sinks can be a nuisance, and the trouble is usually aggravated where solids are tipped down them. If the sink becomes blocked, first try clearing the blockage with a force cup. This may be of rubber or plastic, but the principle is the same.

Block the overflow with a large damp rag. Place the cup over the waste outlet and pump vigorously a few times. A shock wave is set up which usually clears the pipe. If this fails, get a couple of empty buckets handy, then unscrew the plug or section at the U bend. The type will vary according to the age of the unit. In old units it may be a metal plug with two lugs on it, but in more modern plumbing it may be one of a type where a whole section of pipe can be unscrewed.

With the section or plug removed, probe with a piece of curtain wire until the blockage is worked free. Be sure the bucket is under to catch the waste water! Connect up the pipe, then flush through with boiling soda water followed by plenty of cold water.

If this fails too, you may be able to hire from your nearest hire shop a drain clearing tool which connects to a wheel brace.

The illustrations on page 110 also show typical domestic hot water systems, both direct and indirect, and a simple hot water radiator system. Installation does not come within the scope of this book, but it pays to know how each system works, and which stop taps or cocks control which water supply. With hot water systems you will find drain cocks at the lowest points, and it pays to see that these work in case you wish to drain off your system completely—such as when going away for Christmas or a winter holiday. Merely running hot and cold taps will not empty the hot water cylinder to the boiler. This must be removed from the lowest drain cock.

In an emergency, such as a leaking tank or burst pipe, the mains stop tap should immediately be turned off and all hot and cold taps run to empty the storage tank. It is not normally necessary to put a fire out which has a back boiler for, as already mentioned, you won't be able to drain off the water in the hot cylinder from the taps. But you can let the fire die down a little so the water does not boil.

Many people fear an explosion from a back boiler. Such an event is very unlikely unless the expansion pipe becomes blocked or both flow and return pipes become blocked. Far more likely is that you will get poor circulation of water due to furred-up flow and return pipes. If you suspect this, you can buy special descaling kits with which to dissolve away scale without dismantling the plumbing system.

Rusting can occur in central heating systems, especially where new thin wall steel radiators are used. To prevent such trouble, it does pay to add an anti-corrosion liquid to the sealed circuit of the hot water heating system. This can be added by pouring the liquid into the expansion tank in the loft, then draining off water from the lowest drain cock in the system. Hold up the ball valve in the expansion tank until all—or nearly all—the protective liquid has drained into the system. Of course this method cannot be used with any direct heating system.

Finally, do see that all pipes in exposed places are well lagged with proper lagging materials. Include the expansion tank and the overflow pipe. If you have an outside tap, it pays to have a stop tap so that water to it can be cut during winter months. Put lagging over exposed hoppers too, where waste pipes join exposed down-pipes. This is a very common trouble spot. If you can keep the wind off, this will help.

Gas

This is the only part of the book where you are actively discouraged from doing your own maintenance and repair work. Leaks, blockages and other faults are best left to the local gas board to deal with, and they should be notified at once of any trouble.

At the time of writing, two types of gas are supplied in Britain; town gas and natural gas brought in from the sea. Each has its own characteristics of burning and noise, but both are designed to have a distinctive smell before combustion. If you smell gas, find out why.

First open windows to improve ventilation and to disperse any accumulation of gas. Next check that every appliance is off and that no gas at all is being used. Now go to the gas meter and examine with a torch (not a match!) the smallest tell-tale dial which indicates gas is flowing. The dial should be still. If it is moving, even slowly, then gas must be escaping somewhere in the system.

Examine visible joints, and if you suspect a leak, use a strong soapy mix or detergent mix and smear the joints. Gas from a leak will blow bubbles. If nothing can be found, keep windows open and notify your local gas board. They will take prompt action to put matters right.

If a pipe or appliance is found to be leaking, or while waiting for the gas man to appear, turn off the gas at the tap by the meter. When gas is flowing, this tap will lie along the pipe. To turn the gas off, turn the tap so that it is at right-angles to the pipe.

Remember when turning gas on and off to check pilot lights and any appliances in use. Many accidents are caused by a cut supply extinguishing a flame so that when the supply is reconnected the gas is on but not ignited.

Electricity

You can't see it, hear it, or smell it—which is why we find it difficult to understand what electricity is all about. For the same reasons many otherwise competent handymen fear to do anything connected with electrics. True, electricity can be dangerous, but if care is taken, and instructions followed carefully, there is little to fear.

First, get to know what you have got, and here your

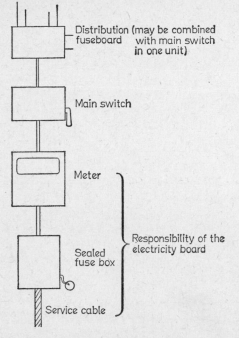

Distribution (may be combined
fuseboard   with main switch
            in one unit)

Main switch

Meter

Responsibility of the
electricity board

Sealed
fuse box

Service cable

responsibility starts where the cable bringing the power to your home enters the main fuse box. You will see this box is sealed, and it must only be opened by a representative from the electricity authority. Cables from this box will go to either a number of separate fuse boxes, each controlled by an on-off switch which usually locks the box shut until the current is turned off, or to a modern consumer unit, with one small on-off switch.

Older properties have the mass of boxes, and if you don't know already, spend an hour finding out which box controls what in the house; the sizes of the fuses and how they fit in the holders. Then draw a plan and pin it on the wall, so that when part of the house develops a fault, you know immediately which box and which fuses will be involved.

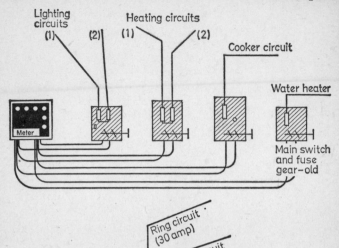

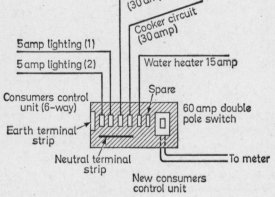

In modern homes, the very compact consumer unit will
contain from two to nine fuses, each controlling one circuit
exclusively. This of course simplifies things very considerably, for trouble can be very quickly located. Again note
the sizes of fuses. On no account should fuse sizes be
changed.

From the fuse boxes or consumer unit, wires will connect

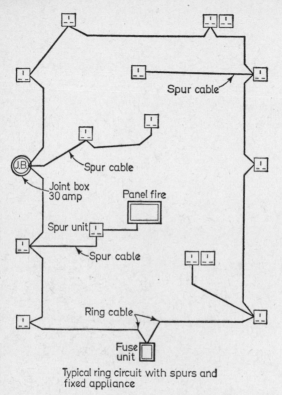

Typical ring circuit with spurs and
fixed appliance

to two main circuits. The lighting system, and the power
system. There may be separate cables to an electric cooker
or to electric storage heaters, but in the main there are two
circuits, and faults on one should not affect the other.

In recent years there have been quite dramatic changes
in the power circuit, for instead of individual cables branch-
ing out to feed individual sockets, a complete ring of cable
is formed starting at a 30 amp fuse, running around the
house, then returning to the same 30 amp fuse. Socket

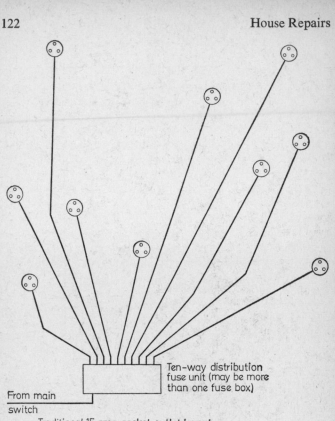

Ten-way distribution
fuse unit (may be more
than one fuse box)

From main
switch

Traditional 15 amp socket outlet layout

outlets and spur units are connected to this ring, giving
a very compact, efficient system.

Plugs and sockets will vary with the age of the house. In
older properties plugs will be found with round pins, in
three sizes—2 amp, 5 amp and 15 amp, while in newer
properties you will find one size of flat pin plug, or 13 amp
plug as it is called. All ring circuits will be wired with 13
amp sockets.

To take the round pin first, the 2 amp plug is for small appliances of less than 500 watts. The 5 amp will take up to 1,000 watts, and the 15 amp up to 3,000 watts. You will find that most appliances carry a plate indicating the wattage, so there should be no chance of your running a two bar fire from a 2 amp plug. The round pin system tends to be abused, for many homes carry multi-adaptors, into which a profusion of plugs are pushed to feed today's accepted appliances. If such a situation exists in your home, it is time to put in new socket outlets to spread the load.

With a 13 amp system, even though all the plugs are the same size, they are designed to be fitted with fuses of different ratings, depending upon the use of the plug. Today there are only two sizes—the 3 amp and the 13 amp, and these will cover all modern appliances. The 3 amp fuse is coloured blue and is for appliances of less than 750 watts. The 13 amp fuse is brown, and is designed to take all other appliances.

So, when wiring up a new appliance, do ensure that the plug carries the correct fuse. Don't assume that it has been sold to you with the correct fuse inside. Check—and keep spares.

When a fuse blows, the first job is to try to establish why it went. Maybe too many appliances were plugged into one socket outlet, and the fuse wire just melted under the load. In which case, pull out the appliances and don't overload again. Or maybe a fault in the appliance or in the flex connected to it caused a short circuit—in which case the fuse can go with a bang. Remove the appliance and don't use it again until the fault has been remedied.

In some older properties, fuses just get tired or corrode away for no apparent reason, and here replacement with new wire is all that is necessary.

Be prepared for trouble, and whether you need fuse wire for fuse holders, or cartridge fuses for modern plugs, have spares to hand. Keep them together with a torch that works,

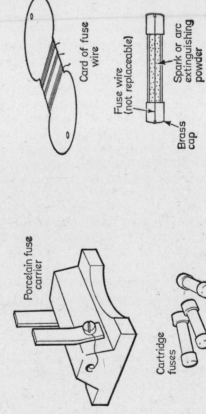

Card of fuse wire

Fuse wire (not replaceable)

Spark or arc extinguishing powder

Brass cap

Porcelain fuse carrier

Cartridge fuses

an electrician's screwdriver, a couple of candles and some matches. The latter are useful when you need both of your hands and you haven't one left for the torch!

With round pin plugs, when a fuse goes, find the appropriate fuse box, turn off the power and remove the fuses one at a time and examine the wire. When a holder with melted wire is found, check how the wire was threaded, and its gauge. Select a piece of similar wire from your card and re-thread. Push the fuse back, shut the box and switch on. If the fuse blows repeatedly for no apparent reason, call in an electrician.

If there is a failure in a 13 amp system, for lighting you will have to go to the consumer unit, switch off; pull the lighting circuit fuses and switch on again. Modern cartridge fuses have the disadvantage that you cannot see if they have blown, so put in a new fuse, then check the old one at your leisure by rigging up a simple circuit with a torch battery, bulb and a piece of wire. If the bulb fails to light, the fuse has gone.

If an appliance fails, check the fuse in the plug connected to it. Again there will be nothing to see, so put in a new fuse, then test the old one. Do be sure to correct any fault before plugging in again. If the appliance still fails to operate, check the fuses at the consumer unit.

When rewiring lamp holders, lamps or other appliances, a good general rule is to make a simple diagram of which wire was connected to what before you remove them completely. Then wire up in the same way. This applies also to switches where a confusion of wires may be connected and looped in.

Rewiring plugs or wiring new plugs calls for care, but it is not a difficult job. The big essential is to ensure that the correct wire is connected to each terminal, and on no account should an appliance needing a 3 core flex be wired to a 2 core flex, ignoring earthing. Many modern appliances are what is called double insulated, which means the electrical mechanism is completely isolated from the user. In this case only two wires are necessary, and no earth need be connected.

You may find that old appliances are wired with a flex having red, green and black wires. This is the old colour coding, with red for live, green for earth and black for neutral. We now conform with the rest of Europe, and the

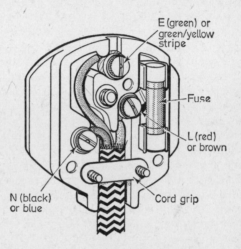

E (green) or green/yellow stripe

Fuse

L (red) or brown

N (black) or blue

Cord grip

new colours are: brown for live, yellow and green stripes for earth, and blue for neutral. So don't be too confused if you have to convert from one to the other.

Round pin and flat pin plugs are wired similarly except for the connection to live in the 13 amp plug. You will see that the fuse separates the actual pin from the wired connection so that if the fuse blows, the current is cut off. Note that the earth pin wire needs to be longer than the other two wires—and you will also see that the earth pin is made slightly longer than the other pins so that earth connection is made first.

Bare just enough of each wire to wind around the appropriate terminal, and wind the wire clockwise so that the screw does not 'unwind' the wire when you tighten it. And don't overlap the wire over itself, or pressure may make it cut into itself, weakening the connection. Don't cut back any more of the flex cover than necessary. It should be trapped firmly under the retaining strap or flex clamp. This clamp is designed to take any strain on the plug, thus preventing the strain being taken by the wires around the terminals.

Give a final check that brown (or red) goes to L, that green and yellow striped (or green) goes to E, and that blue (or black) goes to N. See that the correct fuse is in place (if there is one), then screw on the plug cover.

Take care of all flexible cables, especially those connected to well used appliances such as irons. At the first sign of fraying or bad kinking, cut back or replace the flex. When working on any appliance be certain to disconnect it from the power supply! Don't be satisfied with just switching off at the socket in case it is incorrectly wired. It is possible that some switches cut the neutral wire when the switch is operated, so that power still reaches the appliance, even though it cannot light up or operate. Pulling the plug ensures the appliance really is isolated. Such switches should be re-wired correctly so that the live wire is isolated when the switch is operated.

With lamps and radios and similar apparatus, keep flexes as short as is possible, or wind up surplus on to a card or plastic holder. Don't drape flexes across the floor where people can trip over them. With appliances such as power tools which need plenty of flex, rig up a plug and socket with plenty of flex between and use this as an extension. All power tools must be correctly earthed unless of the double insulated variety—especially if used out of doors.

Because of the complexity of some house wiring, if you do get into difficulties, be sure to call in expert advice. And if the wiring is more than 20 years old, consider having

complete rewiring, because flexes and cables are probably
brittle and perishing. This is the best time to have an old
system modernised.

Drainage

You could say that your drainage system really starts at
roof level, where gutters convey rainwater to down pipes.
Chapter 2 dealt with cleaning and repainting them, but bear

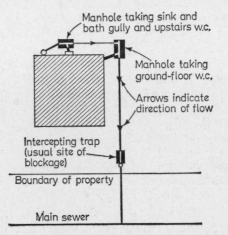

in mind that where these items are in really poor shape, you
can buy excellent plastic rainwater goods which don't need
painting—unless you want to paint. They don't rust or
corrode, or encourage mould growth, and above all, they are
very light and easy to handle. Items are designed to clip or
slot together to simplify fixing. Any good hardware shop or
plumbers' merchant will give you leaflets showing the range
of items available and methods of fixing.

Apart from down pipes, you will see on most older
properties other pipes emerging from the walls. There will
be waste pipes from bath and basins, probably discharging
into an open hopper connected to a down pipe which in

turn is positioned above a gulley into which waste water discharges. There will also be a soil pipe with a vent at about eaves level. This is connected to the main drain and waste from the toilets discharges into it.

In more modern properties, all this tangle of pipes will have disappeared apart from a short length of soil pipe projecting from the roof. The rest of the system is tucked in the walls, out of sight. This is what is called a single stack system, and with such a system, everything discharges into the one main stack. Sanitary fittings and their outlets have to be very carefully sited if such a system is to work properly.

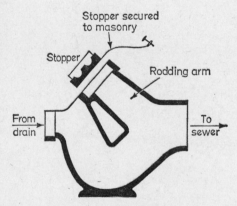

But once the pipes reach ground level, there is very little difference in design. The illustration shows a typical layout, with waste outlets connected to the drain, and the drain sloping down towards the sewer in the highway. There will be heavy manhole covers situated at strategic junctions, and these cover the inspection chambers. It pays to lift these covers from time to time and have a look inside. Accumulated grit and rubbish should be hosed down, and the cement rendering checked for damage or cracking. Get someone to flush toilets and run taps so that you can watch the water flow.

In the final inspection chamber there will be an intercepting trap with a stopper in it. This trap keeps sewer gases and rats at bay, and it is at this point in the drainage system that most blockages occur. The stopper covers a short length of pipe which by-passes the trap. This is called the rodding arm, and it is into this pipe that drain rods are pushed to clear an obstruction.

When a blockage occurs, it is not easy to find or remove the stopper, so it is a good idea to anticipate trouble and fix a piece of stout wire to the stopper, then anchor the other end of the wire to the brickwork. Should a blockage occur, you can heave on the wire and the stopper will come out.

Incidentally, you are responsible for the drain up to the point it joins the sewer. After that, it is the responsibility of the local authority.

It is a good idea to invest in a set of drain rods. Chimney sweep rods will do, and all you need to add is a 4 inch rubber plunger which can be screwed to the end of the first rod.

A blockage can usually be located by lifting the manhole covers and noting which one is full. Obviously if the first chamber is full, then the next one down the line is clear, the blockage must be between these two.

Rods are added as they are fed into the blocked area, and remember always to turn clockwise. If you forget and turn the other way, the rods may part company in the drain, and then you have got trouble!

When a drain runs clear, flush with plenty of hot soda water, then run taps and flush toilets. Before the covers are replaced, clean out the recess around the frame, and put in a little grease so that the cover beds down and gives a practically airtight joint.

Gulleys around the house also deserve a regular clean. An old soup ladle no longer in service is useful for scooping mud and silt from the U traps, then finish off with your hand in a rubber glove. Scrub the grid too, but if it is completely clogged, the simplest way to clean it is to drop the cast iron grid on a bonfire and burn it clean. This applies particularly to grids beneath the sink waste pipe which may get clogged with vegetable matter. Give this grid a regular clean, and flush the gulley with hot soda water and disinfectant to keep it sweet and fresh.

To summarise, check all gulleys, inspection chambers, gutters and down pipes periodically. This way you will minimise the chances of blockages.

12 Twenty simple jobs around the house

Apart from the many larger repair and maintenance jobs about the house, there are a number of smaller ones which crop up in the best-run households. The following are probably the most common. Try to deal with the more minor things as they crop up, for it is amazing what you can learn to live with, given time.

Squeaky Stairs

Locate the squeaking stairs by walking up and down them slowly while a second person takes notes—or, if possible, stands under the stairs making marks.

If you can get under the stairs, you will see that special wedges hold the treads and the risers in place. These wedges can shrink away, allowing the parts to move—and thus

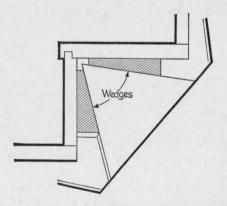

squeak. Pull out loose wedges, clean off all old glue and apply new. Tap the wedges firmly back until they will not move. Allow the glue to set.

If you cannot get under the stairs, put a screw through the tread so that it goes down into the riser. Screw up really tight. You will probably hear the tread groan for the last time as pressure is applied. A little talc or french chalk puffed between gaps will act as a lubricant further to reduce noises from rubbing. Apply screws wherever necessary, and be sure to take the heads down flush with the wood so you don't wear the underlay or carpet.

Scratches on Furniture

Dealing with scratches is not easy today because of the very many finishes available. So you must first try to find out what material you are dealing with.

Turpentine softens ordinary varnishes, and methylated spirit softens shellac finishes. A little of the right solvent applied to the crack with a fine camel hair brush will dissolve the finish into the crack. Next you need some fine pumice powder with which to rub the area smooth. Leave the repair for a couple of days to harden, then polish with wax polish.

If the furniture has been lacquered, you can apply lacquer thinner which, in this case, will act as the solvent. Then treat as already mentioned.

Where a scratch goes right through to the wood, you can often hide the damage by applying coloured stick shellac which has to be melted into the damage. A soldering iron will do to dissolve it, then finish off with the handle of an old teaspoon warmed over a gas burner. When dry, rub with very fine steel wool.

Wax polished timber which has been scratched can be treated with a matching shoe polish—but bear in mind that the polish may go a shade darker than you expect. Experiment first.

Scrape marks and scuff marks—as made by shoes—can

often be lifted out with very fine steel wool lubricated with paraffin.

Where finishes are in a bad way, don't despair. There are french polishes and varnishes designed especially for d-i-y use, and full instructions are supplied.

If you have an epoxy-based synthetic finish on your furniture, it will look wonderful until damaged. Then, there is no solvent for this type of material, and the only successful way of getting a surface renovated is to arrange for the item to be returned and re-coated. This point is well worth bearing in mind when you buy new furniture.

Damaged Fire Backs and Bricks

Before a new heating season starts, examine the fire back and the fire bricks either side of the grate for cracks. Once there are cracks, be sure to deal with them before they get too bad. The fire bricks should be wiggled out, and any number noted. This is usually an impression in the acutal brick. Take this number—or the brick, if there is no number, to your hardware store or builders' merchant for replacements.

While the bricks are out, examine the fire back. Dig out all loose and crumbling material, damp the cracks with water and fill with a good fire cement designed for this job.

Have a look under the grate too, and similarly fill cracks found there—after thoroughly sweeping out all dust.

Plugging a Wall

The simplest way of drilling a wall is by means of a power tool fitted with a special masonry drill, but if you have no drill, a wheel brace fitted with the masonry drill will do, but it will be harder work. Make sure the drill is slightly larger than the shank of the screw. This is allowed for in the numbering of drills, for a No. 8 drill will drill a hole large enough to take a No. 8 screw—and so on.

Make sure that the hole goes well into brickwork or other masonry. The surface plaster cannot take loads—you will merely pull it off. And the hole must be about $\frac{1}{8}$ inch to $\frac{3}{16}$ inch deeper than the length of screw that will be in the wall.

The actual plugging can be a fibre or plastic plug if the hole is of good shape—of the same number as the drill. Where holes are irregular, or merely as a good alternative, use an asbestos fibre filling compound. This is pressed into a hole with a small tool provided.

For hollow walls and partitions, the above methods will not do as the fixing material will merely drop into the

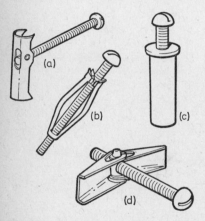

Fixing devices for hollow or thin materials
a, gravity toggle
b, Rawlanchor
c, Rawlnut
d, spring toggle

cavity. In such situations, use one of the special cavity fixing devices which give a firm grip. The types available are illustrated. Most of them cannot be withdrawn without part of the fitting dropping into the cavity, so be sure to assemble whatever has to be fixed before inserting the holding device in its hole.

Broken Ornaments

While there are alternatives, epoxy resin adhesive is probably the best all-round repair material for glass, china and metal ornaments. This adhesive sets by purely chemical action, and once set is unaffected by normal temperatures, by household chemicals or water. Remember that once equal parts from each tube—resin and hardener—have been mixed, nothing will stop the material hardening off. So don't mix more than you need. Rather mix less, then make up more. It only takes a few seconds.

Make sure all surfaces of the ornament are clean and dry, then apply adhesive thinly to both surfaces. Match up the pieces and press until adhesive exudes from the joints. Use transparent adhesive tape to hold the pieces together, then place the item in a warm spot—such as above a radiator. The adhesive will cure in about 12 hours. Providing you can hold the pieces firmly, setting can be speeded up by putting the ornament in a warm oven. Full details of temperatures and setting times will be given with the adhesive pack.

When set, trim off surplus adhesive with a razor blade, taking care not to scratch the surface of the ornament.

Rusted Hinges

Never force a hinge that has rusted up. Something will have to give—and it may not be the hinge joint! First apply easing oil and rust solvent. There are a number of proprietary materials available. Don't be impatient. Give the oil plenty of time to loosen the rust, then ease the hinge very slowly back and forth until it moves easily.

Apply a fine wire brush to the hinge to remove all loose material. Be sure to wear some form of eye protection when doing this job. Rub clean and dry with a lint-free cloth then coat the hinge with a good rust inhibitor. When hard, you can paint.

If the hinge is outdoors, apply grease to the joints. Oil is not much good as it soon evaporates off. Wipe off all surplus grease before the children find it!

Where a hinge just won't respond, take it off and replace —without trying to force it.

Sticking Drawers and Runners

Rub down all running surfaces with fine glasspaper, then treat the wood with wax. A candle stub is ideal, and all you need do is rub this along the running surfaces. Be very careful once runners are greased for the drawer that once had to be heaved may well shoot out.

A modern alternative to wax is a silicone-based wood lubricant now available in aerosol form. This is sprayed on and allowed to dry, after which its effect will last for years.

Sticking curtain runners should not be oiled because of the risk of getting oil on the curtains. Apply wax polish to the rail, and rub with a clean duster.

Lubricating Locks and Bolts

Like all pieces of metal mechanism, locks and bolts need lubrication. With cylinder locks on doors, never apply oil from a can. The oil attracts dust and dirt which may eventually clog the mechanism. If you only have oil, apply just a little to the key, then turn this in the lock. Far better use a graphite powder in a puffer pack. This lubricates without ever becoming sticky.

Mortise locks are best removed, opened very carefully so you don't get springs flying out, then treated with grease or vaseline. You may need to clean off any grease that has become dirty. This type of mechanism is not so delicate, so it can take grease.

Bolts should be oiled, then wiped clean of any surplus. Outdoor bolts will need greasing as oil would evaporate. Always be sure to wipe off surplus lubricant because of the risk of users getting it on hands and clothes.

Rusted Nuts and Bolts

This is a common problem when dismantling outdoor buildings or other constructions which have nuts and bolts exposed to the elements. First apply an easing oil and rust solvent and give it hours to soak in. Apply a spanner which

fits tight, and give part of a turn as if tightening before trying to loosen. This will break any rust holding still.

Often, the bolt will turn in the wood. In this case, hold
the bolt head with a Mole wrench. If you can't get a grip,
cut a slot in the bolt head with a small hacksaw so that you
can get a screwdriver in the slot.

Where a nut is too badly rusted to respond, cut through
it with a steel chisel and hammer until it splits apart on one
side.

If you have a lot to do you can invest in a small tool
called a nut splitter which will effectively cut through a nut
without doing any damage to the bolt.

When replacing nuts and bolts, apply plenty of grease
to the threads. It will preserve the nut and bolt and make
dismantling that much easier next time.

Chipped Basin or Bath

If a china or vitreous surface is damaged, accept at once
that anything you do will only be a form of disguise. If a
chip is knocked out, try to keep it in one piece—and keep
it clean—then stick it back with epoxy adhesive.

If the piece is missing, try to get a paint coating called
a porcelain finish, or choose a matching polyurethane paint.
Apply in very thin coats, coat on coat, allowing each to
dry before the next is applied. A thick coat will droop or
drip. Stop applying when the repair is level with the surrounding surface.

There is little you can do about a crack as dirt will get in
the finest crack, leaving a visible line. You can protect a
cracked basin until it is repaired by applying glass fibre
and resin to the hidden part of the basin in the form of a
patch. Get the unit replaced as soon as possible.

Warped Doors

A cheap door may warp as its moisture content adjusts
itself, or you may get warping through painting one surface
of a door and not another so one can absorb moisture while

the other cannot. You can often improve matters by forcing the door in the opposite direction to the warp and holding it there under pressure.

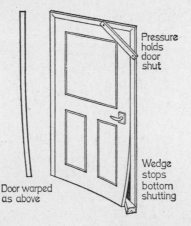

Pressure holds door shut

Wedge stops bottom shutting

Door warped as above

Note which part of the door touches the frame first. Put a block in the door at this point to prevent it shutting, then force home the end that wasn't getting home, and wedge it in place. Leave for as long as possible, and you will find that the door will have lost some of its warp. Repeat until corrected.

Immovable Screws

If a screw cannot be removed, stop before you ruin the slot! Is the slot clear of paint? If not, clean it out so a screwdriver of the correct size will fit. If it won't turn, try a screwdriver bit in a brace. Watch carefully to see you don't do any damage, for this method applies very considerable force. If this fails, try applying the tip of a soldering iron to the screw head. This will expand the screw, perhaps breaking any bond. Make sure too that there is no paint holding the actual head in place. Paint is a good adhesive.

If this fails, try turning the screw as if tightening. This

sometimes breaks the hold. And if all fails, select a twist drill that you think will equal the shank diameter of the screw. Put the drill in a power tool or wheel brace, and drill dead centre on the screw head. Eventually the drill will reach the shank and the head will drop away. Now any fitting can be pulled away.

Finally, grip the shank in a Mole wrench and turn it out. If you have no wrench, file flats on the shank and use a spanner.

When next you put in screws, grease them well. They will go in and come out far easier. Don't use soap. It can rust the screw.

Frayed Rugs and Carpets

Don't ignore frays. They rapidly get worse and can be dangerous. If there is little to turn under, buy a latex adhesive of the type designed for carpet and fabric repairs and liberally coat the backing. This will dry to an almost invisible layer which will prevent further fraying. Then trim. If there is some you can turn under, apply adhesive liberally to both surfaces, allow to become tacky, then press the surfaces together.

Alternatively, bind the edge with a self-adhesive carpet tape. This has a protective quick release layer which is pulled off just before the tape is used. Once pressed firmly in place, the adhesive grips very tightly. Various colours are available, so it is possible to match most carpets fairly well.

Where size can be reduced a fraction and you don't wish to turn the carpet because of thickness, treat the edge with latex adhesive, working it well into the backing, then trim off the frayed area.

Woodworm

The woodworm lays its eggs on exposed wood, preferably on rough surfaces such as bare beams and plywood backs to furniture. The small grubs eventually produced do all the damage, as they bore into the wood, where they eat away for as long as three years. When they eventually emerge as adult beetles, it is the flight hole that you find, perhaps with a little pile of wood dust, or frass, nearby. So when you find holes, damage has already started.

For a small attack, you can buy an aerosol injector to feed woodworm killer under pressure into the tunnel of holes. Or you can apply killer by brush, allowing it to soak well into the wood.

If the attack seems rather large, you can hire an industrial spray from many hire companies with which to spray liquid under pressure. Try to avoid build-ups of liquid on ceilings, as the liquid can seep through.

Where an attack seems severe, or if you find bigger holes, be sure to call in expert advice. You can get a free survey from many specialist companies who will advise you what needs doing. Either they will do it, and give a guarantee, or you can buy the materials and do the job yourself.

Broken Furniture Joints

If joints work loose, pull the joints apart, clean off all dried glue and apply new. A pva or resin glue will do fine, or you can use an animal glue providing the joints will not become damp at any time.

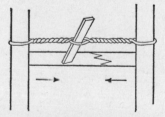

Where rails are snapped, apply glue to both mating surfaces, press the pieces together, then bind tightly. For this job, rubber cut from an old cycle inner tube is fine, as the rubber will take up any contour. A tourniquet of string with a stick to twist it up to give tension will apply force while glue sets.

For outdoor furniture be sure to use a waterproof glue. If none is available, good quality paint is a reliable substitute.

Removing a Picture Rail

In many smallish rooms, removing a rail can add height to a room, but it can be a tricky job because very often the finishing coat of plaster applied to the wall is put on after the rail is put up, so the two levels may not be in exactly the same plane.

First locate the nails holding the rail. These will probably be what are called cut nails. Nails cut from sheet metal, and having considerable holding power. Use a sheet saw or hacksaw to cut through the rail as close to the nail as possible. You can of course use a tenon saw, but mind you don't blunt the teeth on the plaster.

Now lever the rail away from the wall, close to the nail, until you can get the claw of a hammer under it. Protect the plaster with a block of wood so you lever on the wood and not the plaster. The rail will splinter away, leaving the nail in the plaster. Continue in this way until all the rail is out.

Now grip the nails in pliers or wrench or pincers, and wriggle them out. If you try to prise them out with a claw hammer you may bring a chunk of plaster out too.

Brush clean the gap left, damp thoroughly and fill with plaster. *Keenes* cement is quite suitable, and it is far cheaper than using packets of proprietary filler.

Take the filler just proud of the surface, then when set, bring it down flush with a shaping tool or with an abrasive block.

Draught Killing

Special materials are available for preventing draughts, and before a winter sets in, money spent on these materials will be quickly recouped in fuel savings.

Windows can be sealed with foam plastic, supplied with an adhesive backing, or with sprung plastic or metal strip pinned in place.

Internal doors can be similarly treated, while external ones may need an additional weatherstrip along the base to keep wind and rain out. Special rise and fall excluders are available for internal doors so that they will rise over carpets which they would otherwise foul.

Don't ignore external keyholes and letter plates. Special flaps are available for such locations.

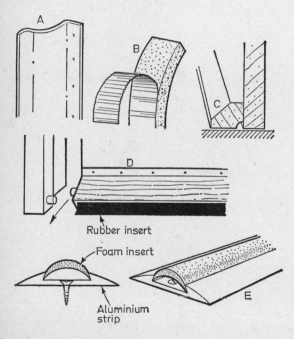

A. Sprung metal or plastic strip
B. Self-adhesive plastic strip
C. Timber weather bar
D. Rise and fall draught excluder
E. Foam plastic under-door strip

Test for draughts at skirting level too, and seal with a quadrant moulding or plastic section. This will make sweeping in corners easier as well. Gaps between floorboards can allow draughts to come up. Any good floorcovering will cure this trouble, or you can seal the gaps as described in chapter 8.

If fires now fail to burn properly, fit a special ventilator over doors so air comes in high where it will be warmed as it enters. Or leave the gap along the top of the door open —to give the same effect.

Smoky Fires

Over-efficient draughtproofing can cause fires to smoke, as no air can be pulled in to feed the fire. The simplest remedy is to give a solid fuel appliance its own air supply by fitting small ventilators either side of the hearth as close to the fire as possible. Ventilators can be bought, or holes bored in the floor can be covered with fine gauze. When boring holes,

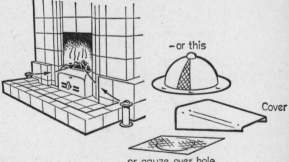

–or this

Cover

or gauze over hole

be careful to avoid damaging gas pipes or electric cables, and mind your eyes when the bit breaks through, as the updraught can be considerable.

Smoking may also be caused by an extractor fan operating in a draught-free house. Air is pulled down flues to replace that being extracted, thus causing smoking. The solution is to give the room a new air supply by means of an openable ventilator. Down-draught may also occur where two rooms are knocked into one, leaving two fireplaces in the room. With one fire lit, air may be pulled down the unused flue to feed the other, and smoke may be pulled down as well.

Tall trees, nearby high buildings, and unusual air currents can also cause downdraughts, and there are special cowls to cure these problems, but some experimenting may be necessary. Reputable companies will advise on types suitable, and they will take back a cowl which does not achieve the desired result.

Panelling a Door

The easiest way to panel a door is to put on a panel of hardboard or plywood which is an inch or two smaller all round than the door. This saves any problems at hinges where a thicker section could stop the door closing. Even so, it is far easier to fix a panel if the door is taken off its hinges and laid flat. If impact adhesive is used, drawing pins can be located at key points to ensure the panel is positioned correctly first go. To play safe, slip a sheet of brown paper, or the silicone treated release paper from the back of adhesive plastic sheeting, between door and board. This will stop the impact adhesive getting a grip before you are sure all is well. With the sheet positioned, pull out the paper.

If the door is covered completely, you need to ease off the moulding against which the door shuts, and re-position it in the door frame. Before finally hammering home nails, check that all is well. If a door seems slightly uneven, shut it, then butt the moulding against it, and pin.

As an alternative to the two coverings mentioned, use laminated plastic. This will give a very durable surface. Woodgrains are particularly effective.

If panel pins are used in plywood or hardboard, be sure

to take them below the surface then spot-fill the holes with a wood stopping.

Killing Rust

Where rust is breaking through a painted surface, be sure to scrape off the paint until the limits of rusting are found. Missing an area hidden by paint may only mean that rusting will continue. Wire brush all loose and flaking rust from a surface, and use emery paper to reduce any build-up. Be sure to protect your eyes during this process.

With loose material removed, wipe clean, then treat with a good rust inhibiting liquid which reduces the rust to an inert compound. Or you can use a cold galvanizing paint which coats the rust with almost pure zinc, preventing any further action.

Once the surface has been treated, paint as soon as possible to prevent further deterioration.

Prevention is better than cure, so treat vulnerable surfaces with an aerosol fine oil protective, with grease or lubricating oil with added rust inhibitor. This applies particularly to tools stored away for the winter, and appliances such as lawnmowers and bicycles.

Small tools, nails and screws can be protected with a special rust inhibiting paper, either by wrapping them in it, or by using containers with lids and with a piece of the paper added.

13 Tools you will need

Quality tools are always a worthwhile investment for the man who plans to maintain his own home. Never buy cheap tools. They last no time, will not retain a good cutting edge, and they can be positively dangerous if something snaps or breaks. So the secret is to add gradually to your kit, getting the basic things first, then extending as other projects are tackled.

And when you have good tools, take care of them. Keep cuting edges keen, for it is usually the blunt tool that slips and causes damage. Apply oil to bright metal to prevent rusting, store them in racks or holders so that cutting edges cannot touch. Get saws and drills sharpened as soon as necessary at a good tool shop, and learn how to sharpen and hone chisels and plane irons. If you cannot sharpen plane blades, invest in a plane with disposable blades.

Below are lists which should prove helpful. Study carefully before buying, and bear in mind whether you plan to have power tools in your kit. A number of hand tools will not be required if you are using power.

Basic Tools

1 foot steel rule
10 foot steel tape
6 inch try square
Cross cut handsaw (7 points to the inch)
Tenon saw (about 10 inches long)
Hacksaw for metalwork
Plane with disposable blades
Wheel brace and set of twist drills

Screwdrivers, small and large, with plastic handles
Electrician's screwdriver with insulated handle
Woodworking vice
Pincers
Pliers, square nosed
Pliers, fine nosed for delicate work
Claw hammer
Selection of bevel edge wood chisels $\frac{1}{8}$ inch to 1 inch
Marking gauge
Marking knife
Chain wrench for pipe work
Oil stone (double sided) and oil
Countersink bit
Masonry plugging tools
Masonry drills, Nos 8 and 10
Self-grip wrench
Adjustable spanner

Extra Tools

Nail punch
Adjustable bevel
Spirit level, long as possible
Small cross cut saw (10 points to the inch)
Jack plane
Router plane
Spokeshave
Brace and a set of bits
Spiral ratchet screwdriver
Pozidriv screwdriver
G-cramps
Sash cramps
Fine pin hammer
Club hammer and cold chisels
Bolster for cutting concrete slabs and bricks
Shaping tool
Glass cutter (wheel type)
Trowel

Hawk
Wood float
Smoothing plane
Mallet
Rubber-faced hammer
Surveyor's measuring tape

Special Tools

Rebate plane
Combination plane
Expansive bit
Hole saw
Dovetail saw

Power Tools

Electric drill, preferably variable speed
Disc sander
Orbital sander
Drum sander
Wire brushes
Circular saw
Jig saw
Speed reducer
Paint spraying attachment
Mortiser
Dovetailer
Rotary rasps

Decorating Tools

Paperhanger's scissors
Paperhanging brush
Paste brush
Plumb line
Pasting table
Foam paint roller
Mohair paint roller
Lambswool paint roller

Pad brushes
$\frac{1}{2}$ inch, 1 inch and 2 inch paint brushes
Blowtorch
Broad stripping knife
Shave hooks
Skarsten scraper
Putty knife

There may be tools here you have not heard of before. A chat in any good tools shop will soon put you wise as to their uses and their value to you at the time. And of course new tools are being introduced all the time. The handyman is always on the lookout for new ideas, but he is also wary of gadgets for the sake of it. Which tool kit has not its 'follies'? Items which seemed brilliant at the time, but which never get used. Some, supposed to save time, take so long to assemble or clean afterwards that their value is cancelled out. Others just don't work.

Advice Available

We are fortunate in this country to have official bodies covering many aspects of home maintenance and repair ready to give expert advice for the asking. Below are a few of the most popular ones:

Building

For advice on any aspect of building materials and fittings, The Building Centres, situated in many large cities. Entrance and general advice is free. The London Building Centre is situated at 26 Store Street, Tottenham Court Road, London, W.C.1.

Carpets

Choose from hundreds of large samples at the British Carpet Centre, Carlton Street, London, S.W.1. Carpet is not sold there.

Cement and Concrete

Expert advice on any aspect of concrete work, plus free booklets on particular subjects, is available from the Cement & Concrete Assn., 52 Grosvenor Gardens, London, S.W.1.

Do-it-yourself

Where advice is not available elsewhere, *Do-it-yourself* magazine offers a free advisory service on any aspect of the subject, including legal problems connected with the home. Write to Readers' Problems, Do it yourself, Link House,

Dingwall Avenue, Croydon CR9 2TA. Please enclose a stamped, addressed envelope.

Electrical Work

For advice on electrical work, rules and regulations, and for free literature, contact the British Electrical Development Association, 1 Charing Cross, London, S.W.1.

Glass and Glazing

Information on glass types, weights and uses, how to glaze, special glasses and mirrors is available from the Glass Advisory Council, 6 Mount Row, London, W.1.

Hardboard and Fibreboard

A complete library of hardboard and fibreboard samples plus expert advice on how to use is available in London. Also useful free leaflets on many aspects of construction work using hardboards. FIDOR, Buckingham House, 6/7 Buckingham Street, London, W.C.2.

Heating

Part of the Building Centres in Britain is devoted to the use of electricity, gas and oil for heating, and advice is freely offered. See 'Building'.

Insulation/Double Glazing

The Insulation Glazing Association offers advice and free literature on double glazing methods—both proprietary and d-i-y. They also offer a list of their members who can help with double glazing systems of all kinds. See 'Glass and Glazing' for address.

Joinery

Most of the windows and doors made of timber used in home construction are available as standard units. For full information on such units, plus details of standard cupboard and unit fittings, write to The British Woodwork Manufacturers Association, 130 Regent Street, London, W.1.

Timber

Where difficulty is experienced in recognising timber, or in locating special timbers, and for advice on timber finishing, contact the Timber Research and Development Association through the Building Centres, or by writing direct to Hughenden Valley, High Wycombe, Bucks.

Wood Preserving

For advice on woodworm and rot control and for information on any aspect of preserving timbers, write to the British Wood Preserving Association, Suite 71, 62 Oxford Street, London W.1.

Index